D0973701

GREAT STORIES
FROM OLD TESTAMENT LIVES

BIBLE STUDY GUIDE

From the Bible-teaching ministry of

Charles R. Swindoll

INSIGHT FOR LIVING

Charles R. Swindoll is a graduate of Dallas Theological Seminary and has served as senior pastor of the First Evangelical Free Church of Fullerton, California, since 1971. Chuck's radio program, "Insight for Living," began in 1979. In addition to his church and radio ministries, Chuck enjoys writing. He has authored numerous books and booklets on a variety of subjects.

Based on the outlines and transcripts of Chuck's sermons, the study guide text is co-authored by Bryce Klabunde, a graduate of Biola University and Dallas Theological Seminary. He also wrote the Living Insights sections.

Editor in Chief:
Cynthia Swindoll

Coauthor of Text:
Bryce Klabunde

Assistant Editor:
Wendy Peterson

Copy Editors:
Marty Anderson,
Glenda Schlahta,
Sue Kimber

Designer:
Gary Lett

Production Artist:
Cindy Ford

Typographer:
Bob Haskins

Director, Communications Division:
Deedee Snyder

Project Manager:
Alene Cooper

Project Coordinator:
Susan Nelson

Project Assistant:
Ellen Galey

Assistant Print Production Manager:
John Norton

Printer:
Frye and Smith

Unless otherwise identified, all Scripture references are from the New American Standard Bible, © The Lockman Foundation 1960, 1962, 1963, 1968, 1971, 1972, 1973, 1975, 1977. Used by permission. The other translation cited is The Living Bible [TLB].

© 1992 Charles R. Swindoll. All rights reserved.

Outlines and transcripts:
© 1990, 1991 Charles R. Swindoll. All rights reserved.

An effort has been made to locate sources and obtain permission where necessary for the quotations used in this book. In the event of any unintentional omission, a modification will gladly be incorporated in future printings.

Notice
No portion of this publication may be translated into any language or reproduced in any form, except for brief quotations in reviews, without prior written permission of the publisher, Insight for Living, Post Office Box 69000, Anaheim, California 92817-0900.

ISBN 0-8499-8428-9

Printed in the United States of America.

COVER DESIGN and ILLUSTRATION: Diana Vasquez

CONTENTS

INTRODUCTION

Everybody loves a good story—one that has enough human interest to hold our attention and enough surprise elements to keep us turning the pages. Great stories wrap us in their scenes and refuse to let us go. Their plots surround us with emotion, and we feel the throbbing heartbeat of each character. As a result, great stories have a way of focusing our thoughts and kindling our imaginations.

In my opinion, there are no greater stories than those contained in the Old Testament. Unfortunately, however, I have noticed that most of the stories God has preserved since ancient days are not being passed down to second- and third-generation Christians.

My hope, then, is that this series will do two things: acquaint the uninformed with some of the best Old Testament stories and whet everyone's appetite for more, so that each person will yearn to rediscover the truths within those accounts that have been covered by the sands of time.

So, let's get started on this new series about old stories. . . . It's one of my favorites.

Chuck Swindoll

Chuck Swindoll

PUTTING TRUTH
INTO ACTION

K nowledge apart from application falls short of God's desire for His children. He wants us to apply what we learn so that we will change and grow. This study guide was prepared with these goals in mind. As you go through the following pages, we hope your desire to discover biblical truth will grow as your understanding of God's Word increases, and that you will be encouraged to apply what you've learned.

To assist you in your study, we've included a section called **Living Insights** at the end of each lesson. These exercises will challenge you to study further and to think of specific ways to put your discoveries into action.

There are many ways to use this guide—in personal devotions, group studies, discussions with friends and family, and Sunday school classes. And, of course, it's an ideal study aid when you're listening to its corresponding "Insight for Living" radio series.

To benefit most from this study guide, we would encourage you to consider it a spiritual journal. That's why we've included space in the **Living Insights** for recording your thoughts and discoveries. We hope you'll return to those sections often for review and encouragement as you continue to grow in your walk with Christ.

Bryce Klabunde
Coauthor of Text
Author of Living Insights

GREAT STORIES
FROM OLD TESTAMENT LIVES

Chapter 1

THE GRUMBLERS WHO DIED OF SNAKEBITE

Numbers 21:4–9

Time is like a book; and somewhere, in some paragraph, you can find your name and the story of your life. You may try to thumb forward in the book, but only God knows the words on those pages. If you're wise, however, you'll flip back and read about the men and women who have gone before you. For their stories teach valuable lessons that can change your present and determine your future.

One of the greatest chapters in the book of time records the history of ancient Israel. And within that history stands one hero, Moses, whose life is a helpful handbook for Christian leaders today. Drawn out of the waters of persecution into a life of Egyptian luxury, Moses went instantly from rags to riches. But those riches were fleeting; for several years later, a flight for his life to Midian returned him to a life of rags. After forty more years, however, he was drawn out again—this time from the desert via God's presence in a burning bush. From shepherding a bunch of sheep, Moses went to shepherding God's chosen people . . . the often straying nation of Israel.

One vignette from Moses' life poignantly illustrates his exemplary leadership skills. It occurred when the beleaguered nation turned on him and the Lord in a place of pain, a place where the harshness of life often drives people to despair. It occurred in the parched wastelands of Palestine's desert.

Understanding the Setting of the Story

The Israelites had become nomads as a result of certain events that began in Egypt, the land of their captivity.

The Exodus from Egypt

Having lived in Egypt for more than four hundred years, the Hebrew people had grown from a small clan in the days of Joseph to a vast nation. But now they lived there in slavery; and their cries of suffering rose to the Lord, who called Moses to lead the people out of Egypt to a land He promised for their own (Exod. 3:6–10).

Pharaoh, however, did not want to release the Hebrews. It took a series of plagues, the last ending in the death of all the firstborn of Egypt, to alter his merciless self-will.[1] Only then, with the death of his own firstborn, did Pharaoh relent and allow the people to leave (Exod. 12:29–33).

Moses then led the new nation out of Egypt, through the Red Sea, to Mount Sinai, where God revealed to Moses the Law which was to govern their nation. Then they hiked to the border of Canaan, where the land of God's promise beckoned.

The Unbelief at Canaan

Poised at the edge of the Promised Land, Moses received new instructions from the Lord:

> "Send out for yourself men so that they may spy out the land of Canaan, *which I am going to give to the sons of Israel*; you shall send a man from each of their fathers' tribes, every one a leader among them."
> (Num. 13:2, emphasis added)

The Lord guaranteed Canaan to the Hebrews; they just had to conquer it. But when ten of the twelve spies returned frightened by the might of the Canaanites (vv. 28, 31–33), the faithless people "grumbled against Moses" to the point that

> the whole congregation said to them, "Would that we had died in the land of Egypt! Or would that we had died in this wilderness!" (14:2–4)

Now really, was it Moses' fault that obstacles stood in the way? He had nothing to do with the high walls and giants in the land. But then, as now, complainers usually focus their fear and anger on leaders, and Moses found himself facing a nation of enraged disbelievers with stones in their hands (v. 10).

---

1. The Jewish Passover originates from this event, with the plague of death passing over the Hebrews who had smeared lamb's blood on their doorposts.

The Wandering in the Wilderness

With His patience toward the grumblers at an end, the Lord stepped in and through Moses told them:

> " 'As I live, just as you have spoken in My hearing, so I will surely do to you; your corpses shall fall in this wilderness, even all your numbered men, according to your complete number from twenty years old and upward, who have grumbled against Me.' " (vv. 28–29)

Consequently, the people wandered in the wilderness for forty years, never entering the Promised Land, reaping the bitter fruit of their grumbling against God.

Analyzing the Plot in the Story

During that wandering period, Moses faithfully led the Hebrews but had to watch thousands die in the harsh desert. Toward the end of that tragic time of death and frustration, Moses directed the nation around the land of Edom toward Moab.[2] On the way the people became impatient and, unbelievably, dared to grumble again (Num. 21:4).

The People's Complaint

Their feelings are understandable, of course, for they had been going in circles in the desert for almost four decades. However, as they voiced their impatience, a familiar tone crept into their complaint.

> And the people spoke against God and Moses, "Why have you brought us up out of Egypt to die in the wilderness? For there is no food and no water, and we loathe this miserable food." (v. 5)

Same song as before. Pastor Moses hadn't caused the sun to beat down; it wasn't his fault the terrain was rough and the food sparse. In fact, it wasn't even his fault they were in the wilderness—their sin brought them there. Yet they targeted him because he was their

---

2. Having just defeated the Canaanite king of Arad (Num. 21:1–3), the Israelites were anxious to continue north into Canaan. But Edom refused to allow passage through their territory (20:14–21). So Moses directed the nation south, back into the desert.

earthly leader; and even more seriously, they launched a bitter attack against their heavenly Creator too.

The Israelites also complained about the Lord's gracious provisions, calling the heaven-sent manna that kept them alive "miserable food."[3] They even criticized God's merciful deliverance from their bondage in Egypt. And with a great crescendo, they then exaggerated their discomfort into a blast of hostility: *We're all going to die in this wretched wilderness!*

Grumble, GRUMBLE, GRUMBLE!

Like vinegar simmering on the stove, their complaining filled the whole house of Israel with a pungent, sour spirit. This wasn't just a minor problem, it was a major problem, and it was poisoning the people. And above all, this toxic grumbling wearied the Lord, who unmistakably declared, That's enough!

The Lord's Response

Without warning or explanation, the Lord sent swift and ironic judgment.

> And the Lord sent fiery serpents among the people
> and they bit the people. (v. 6a)[4]

Symbolizing the nation's poisonous complaining, the venomous snakes slithered into each tent, stinging the grumblers "so that many people of Israel died" (v. 6b). Immediately, they comprehended the sin of their own venomous attitude and pleaded to Moses,

> "We have sinned, because we have spoken against
> the Lord and you; intercede with the Lord, that He
> may remove the serpents from us." (v. 7a)

It has been said that pain plants the flag of reality in the fortress of a rebel heart. This was certainly true of the Israelites; the fiery

---

3. "The venom of the people's anger led them to blaspheme the Lord (v. 5), to reject his servant Moses, and to contemn the bread of heaven. . . . The Lord Jesus speaks of the manna as a type of himself, that he is the true Bread from heaven (John 6:32–35, 48–51, 58). A rejection of the heavenly manna is tantamount to one spurning the grace of God in the Savior." Ronald B. Allen, "Numbers," in *The Expositor's Bible Commentary*, ed. Frank E. Gaebelein (Grand Rapids, Mich.: Zondervan Publishing House, Regency Reference Library, 1990), vol. 2, p. 876.

4. Some have said that "fiery" refers to the burning sensation the snakes' venom caused in the victim, but it probably describes the snakes' reddish color. See John Peter Lange, "Numbers," trans. and enl. Samuel T. Lowrie and A. Gosman, in *A Commentary on the Holy Scriptures*, ed. Philip Schaff (New York, N.Y.: Charles Scribner's Sons, 1899), p. 110.

snakes worked like a purifying blaze, humbling God's grumbling people.

But how would Moses, whom they had just demeaned, respond to their cry for help?

The Leader's Intercession and Solution

With the people on their knees, Moses could have issued a finger-pointing, I-told-you-so lecture. Or he could have scoffed and turned away. However, without a word of condemnation, he graciously and mercifully interceded with the Lord on their behalf (v. 7b).

As a result, the Lord responded to the people's plight, but not in the way they expected.

> Then the Lord said to Moses, "Make a fiery serpent, and set it on a standard; and it shall come about, that everyone who is bitten, when he looks at it, he shall live." (v. 8)[5]

The people wanted the Lord to remove the serpents, but God left the serpents there and provided a remedy instead. Quickly fashioning a bronze snake like the fiery ones at his feet, Moses lifted it high on a pole, and "if a serpent bit any man, when he looked to the bronze serpent, he lived" (v. 9).

Centuries later, that healing look at Moses' bronze snake became the subject of Jesus' illustration of faith for a certain Pharisee. Nicodemus, seeking truth, had come to Jesus at night. And in their lengthy dialogue, Jesus alluded to the bronze snake, saying,

> "And as Moses lifted up the serpent in the wilderness, even so must the Son of Man be lifted up; that whoever believes may in Him have eternal life." (John 3:14–15)

Like the snake, Jesus would be "lifted up" on the cross, bearing the curse of our sin (see 2 Cor. 5:21; Gal. 3:13). And like those who simply looked and lived, anyone who believes in Christ will be saved. What a marvelous cure for the deadly sting of sin! Yet it is both amazing and piteous that so many choose to avert their eyes, dying needlessly.

---

5. Through the image of the snake we see "an exceptionally daring use of potent symbols. As the people had transformed in their own thinking the gracious bread of heaven into detestable food, so the Lord transforms a symbol of death into a source of life and deliverance." Allen, "Numbers," p. 877.

Not only do we see Moses' bronze serpent in the words of Jesus as a symbol of life; but we also see it coiled in the recesses of the temple in Hezekiah's day—as a symbol of idolatry.

When godly King Hezekiah ascended the throne in Jerusalem, almost eight hundred years had passed since the snake incident in the desert. The new king's first order of business was to destroy Judah's loathsome idols—and look what was on his demolition list!

> He removed the high places and broke down the sacred pillars and cut down the Asherah. He also broke in pieces the bronze serpent that Moses had made, for until those days the sons of Israel burned incense to it; and it was called Nehushtan.[6] (2 Kings 18:4)

Completely missing the meaning of the symbol, God's people had been worshiping the symbol itself. So Hezekiah unceremoniously smashed it into pieces. What used to lead people to God now led them to evil, and it had to be destroyed.

The true meaning of the bronze snake, though, will never be crushed. For it is a symbol of God's healing forgiveness, offered to all who, in faith, look to the dying Savior on the cross.

Declaring the Cross from the Story

Going far beyond an interesting account of grumblers in the desert, this story encompasses a world of truth about spiritual life and death. We can point to two broad principles.

First: *By believing in the simple plan of salvation, we live.* Faith in Jesus' atoning sacrifice on the cross provides complete relief and total recovery from the spiritual consequences of deadly sin. If we try to administer our own cure through self-effort, we try in vain. Only by looking at the cross—a small act of belief—can eternal life be ours.

Second: *By worshiping the symbol instead of embracing the reality of its meaning, we die.* We can rub our church traditions and symbols like a lucky rabbit's foot, hoping good fortune will come our way. But religion without a relationship with Christ is tantamount to

---

6. *Nehushtan* is a combination of the Hebrew words for *bronze* and *snake*. It was probably a derogatory name, originated by Hezekiah. See H. Van Broekhoven, Jr., *The International Standard Bible Encyclopedia*, rev. ed. (Grand Rapids, Mich.: William B. Eerdmans Publishing Co., 1986), vol. 3, p. 516.

idolatry. For the programs and symbols become more important than the Person—Jesus Christ.

A Concluding Thought

This story is not so much about serpents and hot sand as it is about sinners in need of healing and recovery, forgiveness and hope. And that is essentially what all the stories we will examine in this series are about. Like Old Testament men and women, we encounter secret sin, pride, depression, greed, grumbling, and fear. But unlike the ancient saints who had only symbols, we see the real thing—the Messiah. And we hear His healing words, "Whoever believes may in Him have eternal life" (John 3:15).

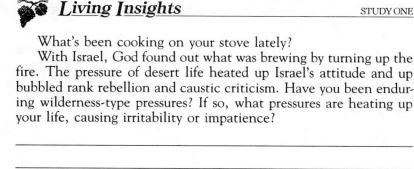

Living Insights   STUDY ONE

What's been cooking on your stove lately?

With Israel, God found out what was brewing by turning up the fire. The pressure of desert life heated up Israel's attitude and up bubbled rank rebellion and caustic criticism. Have you been enduring wilderness-type pressures? If so, what pressures are heating up your life, causing irritability or impatience?

_____

_____

Now take a whiff of what has been cooking. Has your attitude concerning life's difficulties been:

☐ more foul than fragrant?   ☐ more fragrant than foul?

If something is rotten in the state of your attitude, how has that been manifesting itself?

☐ Grumbling   ☐ Moodiness

☐ Complaining   ☐ Criticizing

☐ Pouting   ☐ Rebelling

☐ Withdrawing   ☐ Rationalizing

How can you reverse that sour spirit? Confession was the first step the people of Israel took. They said, "We have sinned, because we have spoken against the Lord and [Moses]" (Num. 21:7). Write out your own confession, stating how you've sinned and whom you've sinned against.

_____

_____

_____

_____

God may be prompting you to share this confession with those you've offended. Start clearing the air today!

🍇 *Living Insights*   STUDY TWO

When God kindled fire to consume His grumbling people, Moses prayed and the fire stopped (Num. 11:1–2). When God sent a disease to punish His rebellious people, Aaron made atonement for their sin, and the plague was checked (16:46–50). So when God disciplined His people with snakes, they cried out to Moses, "Intercede with the Lord, that He may remove the serpents from us" (21:7). Moses prayed, but God did *not* remove the snakes.

Why do you think God chose to leave the snakes among His people?

_____

_____

_____

God offered a surprising solution to the effects of the poison. He ordered Moses to place a bronze snake on a pole and anyone who looked at it would be healed. Why do you think God chose the image of the venomous snake?

_____

_____

_____

Referring to His death on the cross, Christ said, "And as Moses lifted up the serpent in the wilderness, even so must the Son of

Man be lifted up" (John 3:14). How does Christ's death on the cross relate to the bronze snake in the wilderness? Refer to Romans 3:21–26 (especially v. 25), 2 Corinthians 5:21, and Galatians 3:13.

_____

_____

_____

The poisonous effects of sin have stung us all, and without help, we will die spiritually. Yet when we cry for mercy, God does not remove sin from us. Instead, He provides an antidote, which is Christ and His atoning death. Our part is to look to Him, believing that He is the only cure.

Have you trusted Christ to cure the deadly effects of sin and give you spiritual life? If not, use the space provided to express your faith in Christ. If you have trusted Christ for salvation, use the space to express your gratitude that God gave His Son to bear sin's curse for you.

_____

_____

_____

_____

_____

_____

Chapter 2

THE CITY WHOSE WALLS COLLAPSED

Joshua 5:13–6:21

In the boot camp of the wilderness, Israel learned—often the hard way—to trust God as commander-in-chief and, under Moses' faithful leadership, to follow His orders without question. After Moses' death, however, all he had taught them was put to the test, as they stood at the gateway to the Promised Land and faced their most formidable enemy, Jericho.

Strategically, Israel's success or failure in conquering Canaan depended on the outcome of the battle of Jericho. If they gained a foothold here, they could scale the hills up to the Bethel plateau, and thereby separate the northern and southern territories. Their new leader, Joshua, had a divide-and-conquer plan that was brilliant, but there was one major obstacle: Jericho's walls.[1]

An Explanation of the Setting

Earlier, when Moses sent the twelve spies to scope out the land, the Israelites had trembled in fear when they heard the report of Jericho's massive defenses (Num. 13:17–14:1). Years passed, and the nation's confidence in the Lord strengthened; but still they wondered, How can we break through these walls?

From the Human Viewpoint

Every morning when the sun inched over the eastern range, the people watched the light unveil proud and mighty Jericho. They were so close to the land of milk and honey they could taste it; but like David looking up to Goliath, like Moses standing on the shore

---

1. John Garstang excavated the site of ancient Jericho in the early 1930s. He concluded that, "The main defences of Jericho . . . comprised two parallel walls, the outer six feet and the inner twelve feet thick. . . . The outer wall suffered most, its remains falling down the slope. The inner wall is preserved only where it abuts upon the citadel, or tower, to a height of eighteen feet; elsewhere it is found largely to have fallen, together with the remains of buildings upon it." John Garstang and J. B. E. Garstang, *The Story of Jericho*, rev. ed. (London, England: Marshall, Morgan and Scott, 1948), p. 136.

of the Red Sea, and like Jesus' disciples gazing at more than five thousand mouths to feed, they looked up at Jericho's walls and saw towering impossibilities. There was no way under, no way over, no way around, and no way through. For

> Jericho was tightly shut because of the sons of Israel;
> no one went out and no one came in. (Josh. 6:1)

From the human viewpoint, it looked hopeless. But from God's divine viewpoint, this seeming impossibility was just a disguised opportunity for them to see one of His promises come true.

From the Divine Viewpoint

In spite of the strength of Jericho, God promised Joshua:

> "See, I have given Jericho into your hand, with its king and the valiant warriors." (v. 2)

The walls were no problem for God; from His perspective, Jericho was already defeated! But could Joshua marshal the faith to believe God's words? Anticipating this moment of crisis, the Lord had previously prepared Joshua through an encounter with an extraordinary person. Let's look back to chapter 5 and read about this encounter.

> Now it came about when Joshua was by Jericho, that he lifted up his eyes and looked, and behold, a man was standing opposite him with his sword drawn in his hand, and Joshua went to him and said to him, "Are you for us or for our adversaries?" And he said, "No, rather I indeed come now as captain of the host of the Lord." And Joshua fell on his face to the earth, and bowed down, and said to him, "What has my lord to say to his servant?" And the captain of the Lord's host said to Joshua, "Remove your sandals from your feet, for the place where you are standing is holy." And Joshua did so. (5:13–15)

Joshua, the captain of the host of Israel, had met a man of infinitely higher rank—the captain of the host of the Lord.[2] In that

---

2. Joshua was face-to-face with an angel or, possibly, the preincarnate Christ. A temporary, visible manifestation of God is called a *theophany.* See H. L. Ellison, "Theophany," in *The Zondervan Pictorial Encyclopedia of the Bible,* ed. Merrill C. Tenney (Grand Rapids, Mich.: Zondervan Publishing House, Regency Reference Library, 1976), vol. 5, pp. 719–21.

meeting, Joshua learned a valuable lesson: *consecration precedes conquest.* As he bowed low and removed his sandals, he consecrated himself to do battle according to God's will, not his own. Only then was he ready to receive and execute God's plan.

So when God told Joshua that Jericho was his, Joshua believed Him. He had seen the Lord's holiness and might, and he knew that no river was too wide, no situation too difficult and, especially, no wall too formidable for the Lord.[3] Fixing his mind on the power of God rather than the height of the wall, Joshua confidently believed God would fulfill His promise of victory.

An Analysis of the Scene

Rather than trying to fulfill God's promise through his own power, Joshua simply waited for His marching orders.

Instructions from the Lord

Continuing His message to Joshua, the Lord said,

> "And you shall march around the city, all the men of war circling the city once. You shall do so for six days. Also seven priests shall carry seven trumpets of rams' horns before the ark; then on the seventh day you shall march around the city seven times, and the priests shall blow the trumpets. And it shall be that when they make a long blast with the ram's horn, and when you hear the sound of the trumpet, all the people shall shout with a great shout; and the wall of the city will fall down flat, and the people will go up every man straight ahead." (6:3–5)

That's it? To the natural mind that plan sounds illogical. But in impossible situations, God sometimes purposely goes against human logic so that we can't rely on our own reasoning. Besides, the Lord had designed the conquest of Jericho to be nothing short of miraculous.

Obedience of the People

The Israelites didn't have a very good track record where faith was concerned. Joshua must have wondered how they would respond

---

3. Throughout Scripture, God reminds us of His ability to overcome impossible problems. As He said through the prophet Jeremiah, "Behold, I am the Lord, the God of all flesh; is anything too difficult for Me?" (Jer. 32:27, see also v. 17; Luke 1:37, 18:27).

when he explained God's apparently nonsensical plan to them. Would they hesitate? or argue? or doubt?

No, they immediately obeyed. Joshua lined up the armed men, then the seven priests who blew the trumpets, then the ark, and then the rear guard. And they marched around the city once every day for six days (vv. 6–14). As Joshua warned them,

> "You shall not shout nor let your voice be heard, nor let a word proceed out of your mouth, until the day I tell you, 'Shout!' Then you shall *shout!*" (v. 10, emphasis added)

For six days the tension built inside the city as the people of Jericho eyed the unusual parade. Then, on the seventh day, they watched Israel march around their invincible walls once, twice . . . six times. On the seventh time around, "when the priests blew the trumpets, Joshua said to the people, 'Shout! For the Lord has given you the city'" (v. 16b).

Collapse of the Wall

The moment of truth came when the people gave their mighty war cry.

> So the people shouted, and priests blew the trumpets . . . and the wall fell down flat. (v. 20a)

Shouting had never toppled city walls before; but when the cry of the Israelites went up, the walls of Jericho fell down with a roaring crash. Then, still following God's detailed instructions, the Israelites destroyed everything and everyone in the city except Rahab, who had saved the two spies (vv. 21–25).

J. Sidlow Baxter comments on Israel's faithful obedience:

> Faith's first rule of action is to ascertain the will and word of God. Faith's second rule of action is to obey that will and word implicitly. Faith's final rule of action is to reckon on that word, and count the thing as good as done, giving glory to God in anticipation—as the Israelites gave their mighty shout of victory before the walls of Jericho had actually fallen. Faith's principles of action, therefore, cut right across those of natural reason.[4]

---

4. J. Sidlow Baxter, *Explore the Book* (Grand Rapids, Mich.: Zondervan Publishing House, Academie Books, 1960), p. 260.

In faith, Israel had chosen God's way when natural reason spoke against it. And when the walls of Jericho fell down flat, they knew they had chosen well. For God is One who keeps His promises.

Our Response to the Story

The assurance of victory that the Lord gave Joshua sparked hope in a beleaguered nomad nation. As we respond to this story and the promises the Lord gives to us, let's keep in mind the following three truths.

First: *I must remember that God still keeps His promises.* The promises God has given in the Bible number close to 7,500.[5] But they're not just for the likes of Joshua, for "whatever was written in earlier times was written for our instruction, that through perseverance and the encouragement of the Scriptures we might have hope" (Rom. 15:4). That kind of hope is much needed today when we face tough situations. In those times, we can be assured that God still keeps His promises.

Second: *I must be careful which promise I claim.* It is so important to realize that not all the Bible's promises should be claimed personally. Observing the thousands of promises in the Bible, three broad categories stand out to help us decide which promises are for us.

- *Some promises are exclusive.* God told Mary that as a virgin she would conceive and have a child. He told Abraham and Sarah that in spite of their old age they would have a son. He promised peace to war-torn Israel. We can take hope from the way God worked in those lives, but we must not assume that all of God's promises to certain people and groups in specific situations apply to us as well.

- *Some promises are conditional.* God frequently promised to bless His people, but many times those assurances were contingent on obedience. We should be careful not to claim these promises out of context without understanding the conditions for their fulfillment.

- *Many of the Bible's promises are for us.* Although God has not written our names on every promise in the Bible, many of them have us in mind. Philippians 4:19 records one such assurance:

5. Herbert Lockyer, *All the Promises of the Bible* (Grand Rapids, Mich.: Zondervan Publishing House, 1964), p. 10.

"And my God shall supply all your needs according to His riches in glory in Christ Jesus." This is a promise we can cling to, especially during our own Jericho days.

Third: *I must believe and act on God's promises by faith.* Faith minus action is zero. Joshua believed in God's promises, and he immediately and obediently acted out His battle plan and thereby defeated Jericho. Without an active faith like Joshua's, we can have no victory, no comfort, no peace. But faith plus action can tear down even towering impossibilities.

A Concluding Example

Trusting God's promise of victory in your impossible situation and acting on that promise may be difficult, especially if the wall you face is as formidable as Jericho's. But maybe, for the first time, you have seen through Joshua's example a glimmer of hope beyond the wall. If so, look at another example in which a man in distressing circumstances caught a ray of hope from the Lord.

This story, found in the New Testament, opens with a desperate man bringing his demon-possessed son to Jesus because the disciples were unable to cast out the tortuous evil spirit. Jesus asked the anguished father, "How long has this been happening to him?" (Mark 9:21a). And the father replied,

> "From childhood. And it has often thrown him both into the fire and into the water to destroy him. But if You can do anything, take pity on us and help us!" (vv. 21b–22)

Jesus listened intently to the father's words and caught one phrase that sparked His concern. For the father had betrayed his lack of faith when he said to Jesus, "*if* You can." So Jesus responded,

> "'If you can!' All things are possible to him who believes." (v. 23)

Jesus offered the man, who was shivering in doubt, a warm and secure promise. But would he own the promise and clothe himself with it?

> Immediately the boy's father cried out and began saying, "I do believe; help my unbelief." (v. 24)

In a beautiful response of faith and honesty, the man admitted his trepidation but trusted Jesus anyway, even for the faith he lacked.

As a result, Jesus cast out the demon and spared the boy (vv. 25–27), illustrating that all things truly are possible to those who believe.

Are you at the brink of faith, like Joshua and this father—both of whom encountered tremendous impossibilities? Are you lingering there, unsure and fearful, knowing God can do the impossible but also knowing the frailty of your own faith?

Remember, God still keeps His promises to you. Obey what you know to be God's plan, and trust Him for the victory. Your first step of faith may be small as you mouth the words "I do believe"; but know that help from Christ is at hand to take on the impossible.

 Living Insights

"You don't know my problems," some might say. "My spouse is impossible to live with, and my children are impossible to control; my boss is impossible to please, and my bills are impossible to pay. My church will never grow, my aches will never end, my house will never be clean, and my checkbook will never balance!"

Do you ever feel that way? Does pessimism ever wash over you, drenching you with hopelessness and apathy? Record some thoughts about the impossibilities in your life by finishing this sentence:

Sometimes I feel I will never _____

_____

_____

_____

_____

An idealistic solution might be: Flip open your Bible to the first promise you see, repeat it five times, and your problem will disappear. But such a "name it, claim it" approach to God's promises is presumptuous and simplistic.

However, if we err to the opposite extreme, becoming stern realists, we cramp our miracle-working God, for whom nothing is impossible.

The right course is somewhere in between, not simplistic and not closed-minded. The following list of verses contains several universal promises we can claim today. Choose one of these or one you already know from Scripture, whichever promise applies most to your situation, and write it out in the space provided.

Psalm 103:12–14   2 Corinthians 4:16–18
Isaiah 26:3   Philippians 4:19
1 Corinthians 10:13   1 Peter 5:6–7

_____

_____

_____

_____

_____

Now, with God's assurance in mind, take a few minutes to pray for His specific counsel for your situation. If you feel confident of God's direction, write down His marching orders in the following space; then trustingly advance. And remember, God still keeps His promises.

_____

_____

_____

_____

_____

 Living Insights   STUDY TWO

Intimacy with the Lord, as in all relationships, depends on your depth of involvement. A casual brush with Him on Sundays will not produce the intimacy that regular prayer and Bible study bring. But even regular quiet times may not yield much fruit if what you learn is not infused into your life.

One way to live what you learn about God is to develop a journal of His promises you find in Scripture. Keeping and reviewing a log of personally meaningful promises is like building a fire in winter. Each promise stokes your heart-flames until you have a reserve of warmth and security whenever cold winds come your way.

You can start your journal of promises by purchasing a notebook that is divided into sections, so you can categorize the assurances you find. Some categories for your notebook might be:

Promises for a New Week

Promises for Times of Worry

Promises for Children

Promises for Times of Financial Need

Promises for Difficult Situations

Promises for Facing Enemies

Promises for When I'm Sick

Promises for Times of Growth

As you read the Scriptures, always be on the lookout for God's promises to you. Write them down immediately, and soon you'll have a reservoir full of inspiration. And remember to keep it close by for comfort's sake during those blustery days ahead.

Chapter 3

THE MAN WHOSE SIN BROUGHT CALAMITY

Joshua 7

She tried lying on her back. She tried lying on her front. She tried curling up on her side in a tight little ball, but still she felt it! Her host had piled mattress upon mattress to bear her tender frame, yet she tossed fitfully through the night and slept not a wink.

"A nasty, painful lump afforded me no rest at all," she complained the next morning.

"Surely, you *are* a princess," her host exclaimed. "For only a princess has such a delicate composition to sense, at the base of mattresses stacked twenty high, a tiny garden pea."

Hans Christian Andersen's amusing tale of "The Princess and the Pea" illustrates a somber reality. Even the smallest irritant—a seemingly pea-sized sin, for example—can cause us great discomfort. For this is the nature of sin. It always takes its toll on us. Always. And sometimes, as in the story of "The Man Whose Sin Brought Calamity," it takes its toll on many others as well, even an entire nation.

Some Sins Are Silent . . . Others Shout

How can one small sin possibly cause widespread havoc? Isn't sin personal and limited in scope?

It is true that some sins are silent—private between the Creator and His created. But pea-sized or not, sin is sin; and it not only grieves the heart of God, it also obstructs our fellowship with Him. First John 1:5–10 emphasizes this fact.

> And this is the message we have heard from Him and announce to you, that God is light, and in Him there is no darkness at all. If we say that we have fellowship with Him and yet walk in the darkness, we lie and do not practice the truth; but if we walk in the light as He Himself is in the light, we have fellowship with one another, and the blood of Jesus His Son cleanses us from all sin. If we say that we

have no sin, we are deceiving ourselves, and the truth is not in us. If we confess our sins, He is faithful and righteous to forgive us our sins and to cleanse us from all unrighteousness. If we say that we have not sinned, we make Him a liar, and His word is not in us.

This describes sin as a personal problem between us and God. However, as we'll see in the story we will be examining today, sometimes personal, silent sin crescendoes into something more. Like turning up the volume on the stereo from an unnoticeable hum to a deafening din, personal sin can become a blaring, life-shattering, public shout.

Some Days Are Glorious . . . Others, Grim

Today's story tells how one man's seemingly silent sin shouted calamity to an entire nation. As you recall from our previous chapter, Israel had just entered the Promised Land after forty long years of wilderness wandering. Their first military encounter in their new homeland was an earth-shaking success, as they watched the imposing walls of Jericho topple like gigantic dominoes. They must have thought, "Surely the rest of Canaan will fall just as easily."

Then the word *but* enters the story. *But*—what an ominous, bubble-bursting word.

But the sons of Israel acted unfaithfully in regard to the things under the ban, for Achan, the son of Carmi, the son of Zabdi, the son of Zerah, from the tribe of Judah, took some of the things under the ban, therefore the anger of the Lord burned against the sons of Israel. (7:1).

What is this "ban"? Who is Achan? What exactly did he do to so rankle the Lord against Israel?

The answers to these questions will soon become painfully clear. But for now, Joshua and the nation are unaware that something has gone terribly wrong. And they launch out on their next mission, blind to their own peril.

Following the usual plan of action, Joshua sends spies to scope out the next site of conquest—the little city of Ai, an outpost east of Bethel. When they return, they confidently assure him that only a few thousand warriors are needed to take care of this puny opponent (v. 3).[1]

So, without bothering to consult the Lord, Joshua sends a small band of warriors to knock off Ai and then puts his mind to more important matters. But the Lord wants to teach His people a hard lesson, and the Israelite troops have a surprise waiting for them at Ai.

> So about three thousand men from the people went up there, but they fled from the men of Ai. And the men of Ai struck down about thirty-six of their men, and pursued them from the gate as far as Shebarim, and struck them down on the descent, so the hearts of the people melted and became as water. (vv. 4–5)

As the news of the defeat at Ai courses through the camp, a million volts of humiliation stun the people, and their self-confidence shatters like the giant walls of Jericho. Whispers and rumors spread quickly. "Why did God lead us here and then abandon us? Our enemies will think we are pushovers—that Jericho was just a first-round lucky punch. They will be on us in full force, and we won't stand a chance." So Joshua, grieved and confused, does the only thing he knows to do—pray (vv. 6–9).

Like anyone who has experienced a jarring and unexpected defeat, Joshua agonizingly pleads with the Lord to give him a reason for the fiasco. "Why didst Thou . . . deliver us into the hand of the Amorites, to destroy us?" (v. 7). It doesn't occur to him that the hidden cause is sin in the camp. So the Lord plainly tells him that someone has violated the ban He had issued before the conquest of Jericho. And then He informs the commander, "'I will not be with you anymore unless you destroy the things under the ban from your midst'" (see vv. 10–12).

Now it all begins to make sense. Joshua clearly remembers the Lord's instructions, which he had shouted to the people just prior to the fall of Jericho.

> "And the city shall be under the ban, it and all that is in it belongs to the Lord. . . . But as for you, only keep yourselves from the things under the ban, lest

---

1. From Jericho to Ai is an arduous ten-mile hike, an up-and-down, 3,800-foot climb traversing deep ravines and steep inclines. This is why the spies advised against taking a large group up the mountain—"Do not make all the people toil up there" (v. 3).

you covet them and take some of the things under the ban, so you would make the camp of Israel accursed and bring trouble on it. But all the silver and gold and articles of bronze and iron are holy to the Lord; they shall go into the treasury of the Lord." (6:17a, 18–19)

Unknown to Joshua or anyone else—except God—someone has disobeyed that command. But who? And how could just one man's sin affect so many innocent people? For Israel had experienced defeat by association, and so the entire nation suffered. One bad connection had cut off the source of their power, as J. Sidlow Baxter explains:

> The electric wire of fellowship between God and Israel had been cut by "a trespass in the accursed thing"; and the current of power therefore ceased to flow.[2]

Some Reasons Are Clear . . . Others, Confusing

Replaying his memory tapes of the conquest of Jericho, Joshua strains to put all the pieces together. "Was it this person, was it that person? It must have happened when my back was turned." This is agony for any leader, and Joshua feels the weight of his role. "Who could it have been, and why?"

As Joshua wrestles with the problem, on the other side of camp, Achan, the thief, wrestles with his conscience. Does he know the families of the thirty-six men who died at Ai? "Isn't that so-and-so's son? Didn't that other poor man have a wife with a baby on the way?" Achan must have winced inside as he began connecting his sin with the deaths. But as long as the things he took are safely hidden . . . as long as he keeps his mouth shut . . . as long as no one finds out . . .

That night he has trouble sleeping. How can a man sleep well with death on his conscience and contraband in his tent?

Some Consequences Are Personal . . . Others, Public

The next morning, Joshua knows he must assume three roles every leader dreads: prosecutor, judge, and jury. A gloom descends

---

2. J. Sidlow Baxter, *Explore the Book*, 6 vols. in 1 (Grand Rapids, Mich.: Zondervan Publishing House, Academie Books, 1966), p. 260.

as Joshua puts into action the Lord's detailed instructions for identifying and disciplining the sinner.

> "In the morning then you shall come near by your tribes. And it shall be that the tribe which the Lord takes by lot[3] shall come near by families, and the family which the Lord takes shall come near by households, and the household which the Lord takes shall come near man by man. And it shall be that the one who is taken with the things under the ban shall be burned with fire, he and all that belongs to him, because he has transgressed the covenant of the Lord, and because he has committed a disgraceful thing in Israel." (7:14–15)

Through the drawing of lots, the tribe of Judah is picked. Then the family of the Zerahites. Then the household of Zabdi. Then . . .

Achan's mind is reeling. This is impossible. Someone must have seen him in the act. Someone must have betrayed him. As all the men in his family file by Joshua, his eyes are riveted to the lots. When his lot is drawn, the crowd gasps and then hushes in a deathly silence. In a momentary trance, Achan stands without moving, bearing the full weight of his guilt.

> Then Joshua said to Achan, "My son, I implore you, give glory to the Lord, the God of Israel, and give praise to Him; and tell me now what you have done. Do not hide it from me." So Achan answered Joshua and said, "Truly, I have sinned against the Lord, the God of Israel, and this is what I did; when I saw among the spoil a beautiful mantle from Shinar and two hundred shekels of silver and a bar of gold fifty shekels in weight, then I coveted them and took them; and behold, they are concealed in the earth inside my tent with the silver underneath it." (vv. 19–21)

---

3. Since there were no eyewitnesses of the crime, God named the thief through the drawing of lots, the outcome of which He controlled. Keil and Delitzsch describe the possible manner by which the lots were drawn: "In all probability little tablets or potsherds were used, with the names written upon them, and these were drawn out of an urn." C.F. Keil and F. Delitzsch, *Commentary on the Old Testament* (Grand Rapids, Mich.: William B. Eerdmans Publishing Co., 1978), vol. 2, p. 80.

He had seen the Babylonian robe and thought, "What a prize! My tattered clothes are worn and shabby. Why, this new robe is just my size." He had seen the five pounds of silver and the one-and-a-quarter pounds of gold and thought of the wonderful things he could buy. "It has been such a long, difficult journey in the wilderness, surely I deserve a little finery." So privately he took them, and privately he hid them; but now, how naked and public—and obscenely pathetic—his sin appears as the cursed contraband is piled at his feet (vv. 22–23).

The suspect arrested, the confession recorded, the evidence displayed, the sentence pronounced, Joshua has one duty left to perform—the execution. With no plea bargaining, no cry of rights violated, Achan, his children, and all he owns are taken to the valley of Achor,[4] where they are stoned, burned, and morbidly memorialized in a giant mausoleum of stones (vv. 24–26).

Lingering Lessons

Like life, the stories in the Bible do not always have fairy-tale endings. The lessons God wants to teach us are too important to be trivialized; and often, a tragedy is the best way to get our attention. Let's let Achan's tragedy grab us and learn the lesson it offers.

First: *There is a unique stench connected with suspicion.* The closer we walk with God, the more sensitive our "spiritual noses" become, and the more quickly we can detect the stench of suspicious sin. It's a keen intuition from the Lord that tells us something fishy is going on. It can't be explained more than that; and a leader must be sensitive to smell it when there's sin in the camp.

Second: *An absence of peace accompanies hidden sin.* When Achan first stole the robe and the money, he must have felt very satisfied. Maybe that first night he even slept well, dreaming of his spoil, proud of his daring savvy. But the second day, did his treasure begin to tarnish? Did he think of his hiding place every minute? Did it seem to flash in neon: "Achan's sin, Achan's sin"? Hidden sin agonizes the soul.

Third: *When wrong is uncovered, God honors swift and thorough action.* God's ministry is too important for us to allow hidden sin to cut the lines to Him, our only source of power. So, though

---

4. Interestingly, Achan and Achor are from the same root word which means "trouble" (see Prov. 11:29).

spiritual discipline is surely the most torturous duty of ministry, God honors it when it is swift and thorough.

Joshua later went on to conquer Ai, along with most of Canaan. But in spite of his successes, our eyes return to the pile of stones in Achan's valley of trouble. For it reminds us of personal legacies of pain in our own troublesome valleys. And, whichever role we have filled—Achan, the miserable sinner; Joshua, the beleaguered leader; or the people, the innocent victims—we have tasted the bitter cup of not-so-secret sin.

And we stand like mourners at the grave, and we remember.

 ## Living Insights STUDY ONE

Spiritually speaking, the valley of Achor is a midnight maze.

For those who can see, the world of blindness is difficult to imagine. It is not like simply shutting the shades and turning out the lights in your home, for even in the darkness your mind's eye can picture the rooms. No, it's more like fumbling through a human-sized maze in a midnight that has no moon, no stars, no light. That's also what it's like to have unconfessed sin in your heart. When you close your eyes to God's light and guidance, you wind up in a tent with Achan—living through a season of sin-sponsored trouble, where you are disconnected from God and lost in a labyrinth of black confusion.

Isaiah describes this miserable separation and wandering in chapter 59 of his book. Take a moment to read the first two verses.

Have you felt separated from God lately? If so, could it be because of a hidden stash of sin in your life? Search your heart, dig up any stolen treasures, and lay them before the Lord. Write down what you find.

_____

_____

_____

_____

Not only do these hidden sins disconnect us from God, they also cause distress in our lives. In verses 3–8 of this passage the prophet describes the sins of the people, and in verses 9–15 he portrays the results of their sin. Read through those verses three times; on the third reading, write down some possible results of your own sin.

_____

_____

_____

_____

Trouble. In a word, that summarizes what happens when we conceal our sinfulness from the Lord. We grope, we stumble, we growl, we moan, we hope in vain, and we lie to cover our tracks. We enter a valley of Achor.

Mercifully, there is a way out of the dark maze and back into the light. And that is the focus of Study Two.

 ## Living Insights

But the valley of Achor is also a door of hope.

God does not abandon us in our sin-caused valley of trouble. He has even provided the means by which this dark, hopeless maze can become a path toward peace and restoration. The valley of Achor *can* be a door of hope.

In the book of Hosea, the Lord reveals what this door is and how to get through it. Wayward Israel is like Hosea's adulterous wife, and the Lord issues a prophetic warning saying that, as a result of her sin, she will have to experience a black valley of Achor—a period of wilderness wandering and discipline. But God also tells Israel that restoration is possible; hope does exist.

> "Therefore, behold, I will allure her,
> Bring her into the wilderness,
> And speak kindly to her.
> Then I will give her her vineyards from there,
> *And the valley of Achor as a door of hope.*
> And she will sing there as in the days of her
>   youth,
> As in the day when she came up from the land of
>   Egypt."
> (Hos. 2:14–15, emphasis added)

In verses 19–20, God goes on to say that He will betroth Himself to Israel. How does He describe that marriage, and what are the benefits?

_____

_____

_____

Even in the darkest valleys of sin, the Lord extends His forgiving hand. Later in his book, Hosea urges Israel to respond to the Lord's invitation and experience renewed fellowship and peace. See what he writes:

> "Come, let us return to the Lord.
> For He has torn us, but He will heal us;
> He has wounded us, but He will bandage us.
> He will revive us after two days;
> He will raise us up on the third day
> That we may live before Him."
> (6:1–2)

From 1 John 1:9, we know that returning to the Lord takes place through confession—the key that unlocks the door of hope. Conclude this Living Insight using that key of confession. You may use the lines below if you wish, or you may feel that you need to pour your heart out to the Lord on your knees in prayer.

Whatever you do, remember the door.

_____

_____

_____

_____

_____

_____

Chapter 4

THE KING WHO REFUSED TO BOW

1 Samuel 13–15

I have played the fool."

These bitter words from 1 Samuel 26:21 are the self-proclaimed epitaph of a king named Saul who had it all and lost it. He had God's blessing but lost it. He had power and authority but lost that too. He had the love and admiration of thousands but, in the end, died ashamed and alone.

Starting out with great natural abilities and even God's approval, he showed much promise and climbed high with remarkable speed and grace. Then, while he was balancing ever so gingerly on the pinnacle of success, a wind of pride and jealousy toppled him, and down he fell.

What factors brought about his shocking downfall? And, most importantly, how can we avoid such a rooftop slide? These questions concern us; but in order to answer them, we must start our story with the nation Israel and their cry for a king.

A Brief Study of Hebrew Life before Saul Became King

Ever since Moses led the Israelites out of Egypt and Joshua ushered them into the Promised Land, the nation had had no king. God had governed them Himself through His law and His selected leaders. But the Israelites found that arrangement socially embarrassing, because all the other nations had flashy kings. And now that Samuel, their existing leader, was aging and his sons were becoming more corrupt every day (1 Sam. 8:1–6), they demanded of the Lord, "Give us a king!"

Through Samuel, God warned the people that a king would be oppressive, that his taxes and military ventures would sap them of their resources (vv. 7–18).[1] But His warnings bounced off the people's

---

1. Note how many times the phrase "he will take" appears in verses 11–17.

stubborn resolve and, like rebellious teenagers already out the door, they determined to have their own way (vv. 19–20).

So God chose Saul to be the first king of Israel, and this is where Saul's climb up the roof to fame and power began. From a human perspective, he was the best man for the job. He had the image, the style, and the good looks (9:2). Not only that, he was genuinely modest. When Samuel first met Saul and began telling him that God had chosen him to be leader of the nation, he responded,

> "Am I not a Benjamite, of the smallest of the tribes of Israel, and my family the least of all the families of the tribe of Benjamin? Why then do you speak to me in this way?" (v. 21)

Best of all, in the beginning he was in tune with God. He was generous, merciful, and empowered by the Holy Spirit (10:6–7). Even so, Saul did not boast about his anointed position. In fact, at his introduction, he was nowhere to be found! The people finally had to ask the Lord to help find him.

> So the Lord said, "Behold, he is hiding himself by the baggage." (v. 22b)

With a rush, the people ran to his hiding place and grabbed their new—albeit reluctant—hero, proclaiming him king (vv. 23–24). In this way, almost in spite of himself, Saul arrived at the top. And when he defeated public enemy number one, Nahash the Ammonite, the whole nation united in support of their new celebrity (chap. 11).

But in the midst of the cheers and backslapping, his humility gives way to pride. As a result, he allows the vermin of jealousy, impatience, and stubborn rebellion to nibble at his trust in the Lord. Unnoticed, Saul's footing is slipping.

An Analysis of Saul's Tragic Character Erosion

In three instances, Saul's response to stressful situations reveals the cracks in his nature. The first rift is seen when a Philistine invasion puts on the heat and the nation is running scared.

Impatient Offering (1 Sam. 13)

When our story takes place, Saul's son Jonathan and his soldiers have just defeated a Philistine outpost planted in the middle of

Israel. Meanwhile, Saul and his troops have retreated to Gilgal[2] to amass reinforcements and to meet Samuel. Despite the recent victory, the inexperienced Hebrew soldiers are melting with fear.

> When the men of Israel saw that they were in a strait (for the people were hard pressed), then the people hid themselves in caves, in thickets, in cliffs, in cellars, and in pits. Also some of the Hebrews crossed the Jordan into the land of Gad and Gilead. But as for Saul, he was still in Gilgal, and all the people followed him trembling. (13:6–7)

It's a terrifying time, and Saul anxiously waits to hear God's word from Samuel, but Samuel isn't there. With each day that goes by, more and more of his army deserts. Samuel was supposed to come in seven days to make a sacrifice; but when he is late, Saul breaks under the pressure and makes the burnt offering himself (vv. 8–9).

As king, Saul has no right to make a priestly sacrifice. But in the stress of the moment, his fault line of impatience cracks and we see an underlying irreverence and panic. As soon as he completes the presumptuous act, Samuel appears and confronts him.

> But Samuel said, "What have you done?" And Saul said, "Because I saw that the people were scattering from me, and that you did not come within the appointed days, and that the Philistines were assembling at Michmash, therefore I said, 'Now the Philistines will come down against me at Gilgal, and I have not asked the favor of the Lord.' So I forced myself and offered the burnt offering." (vv. 11–12)

Saul doesn't understand that it is always better to wait on the Lord for guidance than to brashly forge ahead without Him. Unfortunately, he learns that lesson the hard way and suffers the consequences of his presumption.

> And Samuel said to Saul, "You have acted foolishly.
> . . . The Lord would have established your kingdom

---

2. Gilgal is important to Saul because of its history and significance. It was where Joshua's forces were camped when Jericho was defeated (Josh. 5–6), where Samuel regularly ministered (1 Sam. 7:15–16), where Saul was made king (11:14–15), and where Samuel had prophesied earlier that he would meet Saul after a seven-day wait (10:8).

over Israel forever. But now your kingdom shall not endure. The Lord has sought out for Himself a man after His own heart, and the Lord has appointed him as ruler over His people, because you have not kept what the Lord commanded you." (vv. 13–14)

God was looking for a "man after His own heart"—a man with unfailing devotion and uninhibited faith. Saul was not that man, for although Saul took his *circumstances* seriously, he didn't take God seriously.

As a result of his unrepentant disobedience, God takes the royal line away from Saul and gives it to another, the shepherd boy David. Saul's standing as the respected leader wobbles, and the next incident undermines his footing even more.

Rash Vow (1 Sam. 14)

After imprudently making the sacrifice, Saul leads what's left of his ragtag army of six hundred soldiers from Gilgal up to the hill country, where he plans to make his last stand—Custer style.[3] The Philistines have rallied at a strategic pass near Michmash, and the upcoming battle looks hopeless for Israel (13:15–23).

With great courage and faith, Jonathan and his armor bearer slip away from the Israelite encampment and slay twenty warriors of a Philistine garrison (14:1–15). This surprise attack spooks the Philistines, and they scatter in all directions. Seeing their confusion, the Hebrews muster their grit and begin to rout their fleeing enemy (vv. 16–23). It's a miraculous victory, but Saul makes a rash, foolish vow that dampens the spirits of the people and almost sentences his own son to death.

> Now the men of Israel were hard-pressed on that day, for Saul had put the people under oath, saying, "Cursed be the man who eats food before evening, and until I have avenged myself on my enemies." So none of the people tasted food. (v. 24)

Unaware of the oath, Saul's son Jonathan finds some honey and eats it. But Saul has spun around himself such a complicated web of fear, arrogance, and paranoia that he will not recant his frivolous command.

3. At the beginning of the war, Saul had thousands of men with him (13:2). Now all that remain are six hundred (v. 15; 14:2).

Then Saul said to Jonathan, "Tell me what you have done." So Jonathan told him and said, "I indeed tasted a little honey with the end of the staff that was in my hand. Here I am, I must die!" And Saul said, "May God do this to me and more also, for you shall surely die, Jonathan." (vv. 43–44)

Fortunately for Jonathan, the people intervene and rescue him from his father's irrational stubbornness (v. 45). Saul, however, never does admit that he made a mistake. His foolishness reveals another crack in his character: Although Saul took *himself* seriously, he did not take God seriously.

How much better it would have been for him to humbly admit the rashness of his vow! That would have won the respect and support of the people. Instead, they become even more aware of the fissures in Saul's foundation. The final rift appears when, once again, he disobeys God's command.

Disobedient Act (1 Sam. 15)

Although the Lord has moved Saul out of the royal line, in His mercy He gives this headstrong leader another chance to regain favor. Through Samuel, the Lord gives Saul clear instructions to punish the Amalekites for their attack on Israel centuries earlier.[4]

> " 'Now go and strike Amalek and utterly destroy all that he has, and do not spare him; but put to death both man and woman, child and infant, ox and sheep, camel and donkey.' " (15:3)

Saul wins the battle; but like a cocky quarterback who changes the coach's plays, he takes matters into his own hands. Instead of total annihilation, he spares a few trophies of his great victory, namely King Agag and his premium livestock (vv. 4–9). Then, on his way back from setting up a monument to himself, who should appear but Samuel. All smiles and sunshine, Saul says, "Blessed are you of the Lord! I have carried out the command of the Lord" (v. 13).

In light of his disobedience, Saul should have been on his knees begging for forgiveness. But not only does he refuse to bow to

---

4. When Moses led the people from Egypt to Sinai, descendants of Esau—the Amalekites—ruthlessly attacked the young nation. With God's help Israel won the battle, but God promised to "utterly blot out the memory of Amalek from under heaven" (Exod. 17:8–16; see also Gen. 36:12).

Samuel in shame, he lies to him as well! He has *not* carried out the command of the Lord, and Samuel immediately confronts him on his deception (v. 14). But Saul rationalizes[5] away his disobedience and even puts the blame on others.

> Then Saul said to Samuel, "I did obey the voice of the Lord, and went on the mission on which the Lord sent me, and have brought back Agag the king of Amalek, and have utterly destroyed the Amalekites. But the people took some of the spoil, sheep and oxen, the choicest of the things devoted to destruction, to sacrifice to the Lord your God at Gilgal." (vv. 20–21)

How pitiful! Saul has convinced even himself that he has done the right thing. He says, "I *did* obey the voice of the Lord." But the truth reveals his sinful heart.

Samuel's eyes narrow as he issues God's sentence of judgment.

> "Has the Lord as much delight in burnt offerings
>   and sacrifices
> As in obeying the voice of the Lord?
> Behold, to obey is better than sacrifice,
> And to heed than the fat of rams. . . .
> Because you have rejected the word of the Lord,
> He has also *rejected you from being king.*"
> (vv. 22–23, emphasis added)

Crash! This third rift of rebellion is the final slip off the rooftop's peak, and down the other side Saul now tumbles. How could he have been so blind to his sin? In this case, although Saul took the *people* seriously, he did not take God seriously.

The rest of Saul's years are spent floundering in paranoia, despair, and regret; and in the end he dies by suicide (31:4). His life is a tragedy, because one can't escape thinking of what it could have been. Yet the reasons for his failure are the same reasons people fail today. He bowed to circumstances, he bowed to himself, he even bowed to others. But he refused to bow to God.

---

5. To rationalize means "to attribute (one's actions) to rational and creditable motives without analysis of true and especially unconscious motives . . . to provide plausible but untrue reasons for conduct." See *Webster's Ninth New Collegiate Dictionary,* "rationalize."

A Few Reminders for All Who Walk with God

By his negative example, Saul's life teaches us four lessons.

First: *To assume you will end strong because you've started strong is foolish.* The true test of character is time. So in order to end well, it is important to not allow little faults in the beginning to grow. Therefore, we should learn to keep short accounts.

Second: *To presume into inappropriate areas because circumstances are uncomfortable is dangerous.* When the heat is on, we sometimes make mistakes we never would have made otherwise. At those times we need to watch and pray.

Third: *To jeopardize the well-being of another because you're unwilling to alter an unwise decision is unfair.* Poor decisions have a domino effect: they tend to trigger a series of foolish actions that will eventually affect others. The key is to stop the process as soon as possible; so it is necessary, early on, to admit and change.

And fourth: *To rationalize your disobedience because you wanted your way is rebellion.* Rebellion against God is most pitiful when, through rationalization of wrong, rebels think they are doing right. Therefore, we must always be sensitive to what is black and white to avoid rationalization's deceptive graying—we must always be willing to face the truth.

The decline of King Saul teaches us to take God's Word seriously. Saul "feared the people and listened to their voice" (15:24) instead of listening to God's. May that never be said of us, lest in the end we admit, along with Saul, "I have played the fool."

 Living Insights

A brooding tyrant resides within us all—our King Saul voice of pride. It is our smooth-talking flesh, the soul's fool. We hear it when God reaches down from heaven and lifts us to a place of honor, and it says, *"I deserved that."* We hear it when others say, "Watch out!" and it replies, *"I can handle it."* And we hear it when we make a mistake and it says, *"It was their fault."*

This King Saul voice in us is our lifelong enemy, but also within us is King Christ—our victorious champion (see Rom. 8:1–11). When we ease back on our laurels, He says, "Remember the secret sins; *keep short accounts.*" When we want to handle tough times ourselves, He says, "Wait for My timing; *watch and pray.*" When we make a hasty decision that injures others, He says, "Be humble;

admit and change." And when we have blatantly sinned, He says, "Be honest about it; *face the truth.*"

Stop now, and think about which voice you have been listening to lately. Has that King Saul voice been more persuasive? Or has King Christ captured your attention?

In the following exercise, imagine Christ's voice giving you the commands. To what situation in your life does He refer? Who is involved? What specifics does He want you to consider? How can you obey? Ponder each point and let King Christ win your attention and your heart.

Keep Short Accounts

_____

_____

_____

_____

Watch and Pray

_____

_____

_____

Admit and Change

_____

_____

_____

_____

Face the Truth

_____

_____

_____

_____

Living Insights

We run into trouble when we confuse the serious with the not so serious. Saul took his circumstances, himself, and others more seriously than he did the Lord. He reacted to those things he should have relaxed about, and he sloughed off the One he should have obeyed.

How about you? Have your priorities been confused lately? Do your actions reveal a misplaced motivation? Think through the following questions, then ask the Lord for wisdom to perceive what should be taken more seriously.

• How does worrying about circumstances short-circuit your faith in the Lord?

_____

_____

_____

• How does taking your image too seriously obstruct Christ's image?

_____

_____

_____

• How does preoccupation with others' opinions of you obscure your interest in Christ's opinion of you?

_____

_____

_____

• If you feel that you have not been taking Christ seriously enough lately, in what ways can you make Him "number one" again?

_____

_____

_____

May the following prayer reflect your commitment to Him.

Use me then, my Savior, for whatever purpose, and in whatever way, you may require. Here is my poor heart, an empty vessel; fill it with your grace. Here is my sinful and troubled soul; quicken it and refresh it with your love. Take my heart for your abode; my mouth to spread abroad the glory of your name; my love and all my powers, for the advancement of your believing people; and never suffer the steadfastness and confidence of my faith to abate; so that at all times I may be enabled from the heart to say, "Jesus needs me, and I am his."

Dwight L. Moody[6]

6. Dwight L. Moody, as quoted in The One Year Book of Personal Prayer (Wheaton, Ill.: Tyndale House Publishers, 1991), p. 9.

Chapter 5

THE PROPHET WHO PRAYED TO DIE

1 Kings 19:1–14, 18–21

The woman's eyes shot angry flames of fire at the paramedics who wheeled her from the ambulance into the emergency room. "Get away from me!" she screamed at an approaching nurse. "You have no right to not let me die! It's my life, and I can do as I please. You can't do this to me!" She struggled violently until finally slipping into unconsciousness.

During the days that followed, the woman calmed enough to reveal her pain. Her mornings had always begun with a "blackness inside so deep that I can literally see it." And through the day "my chest alternates between a dull ache and a weighty depression that makes me feel hopeless and without meaning." Even the comfort of sleep had eluded her, for she often woke at night for no reason and stared at the ceiling until early morning. Finally, she could take it no more.

What's remarkable is that no one knew, for on the outside she had everything. She was a spiritual leader at church, having had the best Bible training, and she had a model home with four loving children and a successful pastor husband. Routinely, she prayed, read the Bible, and met with friends. But nothing eased her feelings of loneliness or dispersed the clouds of depression that settled on her soul.[1]

Discouragement and disillusionment are the twin demons of depression, even for Christians. And Charles Haddon Spurgeon, the great nineteenth-century preacher, found that even spiritual leaders are susceptible. He called their down times "the minister's fainting fits."

> Fits of depression come over the most of us. . . . The strong are not always vigorous, the wise not always

---

1. Adapted from *When Your World Makes No Sense*, by Henry Cloud (Nashville, Tenn.: Thomas Nelson Publishers, Oliver Nelson, 1990), pp. 11–12.

ready, the brave not always courageous, and the joy-
ous not always happy. . . .
. . . Such was my experience when I first became
a pastor in London. My success appalled me; and
the thought of the career which it seemed to open
up, so far from elating me, cast me into the lowest
depth. . . . Who was I that I should continue to
lead so great a multitude?[2]

These same words could have been spoken by another great
minister of old who experienced a "fainting fit"—the prophet Elijah.
Grappling for his life with the devil Despair, he also entered depression's darkness. The Lord then came to his rescue and lifted him
out of that pit. But how did God's man fall into such discouragement? It all began when he stepped out to confront Israel, God's
wayward people.

The Setting of the Story

Ahab and Jezebel, Israel's king and queen, were worshipers of
Baal (1 Kings 16:29–33). And because of their wickedness and their
evil impact on the nation, God ordered a drought on the land
(17:1). But He also wanted the nation to repent and worship Him,
so He planned a showdown between His man Elijah and 450 prophets of Baal. The false prophets prepared a sacrifice and prayed for
Baal to send fire down to devour it. But the heavens were silent
until Elijah prayed. The Lord immediately answered his prayer,
torching the sacrifice, the wood, and the altar. Amazed, the nation
bowed down to the Lord in fear. And soon after, the skies opened
and the rains drenched the parched land (chap. 18).[3]

A Henpecked Husband (Ahab)

Frightened and worried, Ahab scurried home to "Mama"—his
wife, Jezebel. With a sniveling whine, he tattled on Elijah, the
meanie who had embarrassed him and destroyed all their prophets
(19:1). Like many husbands who are controlled by a domineering
wife, he fell apart under pressure, reverting to the role of a child.

---

2. C. H. Spurgeon, *Lectures to My Students* (n.d.; reprint, Grand Rapids, Mich.: Associated
Publishers and Authors, 1971), pp. 167, 173.

3. Baal was the Phoenician fertility god of rain and thunder. In this passage, God proves His
power as the true and living God of the world, including Baal's supposed domain (see 18:1).

A Domineering Wife (Jezebel)

Jezebel soothed her little man while her anger boiled against Elijah. Turning quickly to Ahab's defense, she took matters into her own hands and issued her edict.

> Then Jezebel sent a messenger to Elijah, saying, "So may the gods do to me and even more, if I do not make your life as the life of one of them by tomorrow about this time." (v. 2)

A Brokenhearted Prophet (Elijah)

And what is Elijah's response? He had just faced an entire nation who opposed him; he had personally executed the 450 prophets of Baal (18:40); and he had waited for rain on a cloudless day, and torrents had flooded the earth. He had even raced Ahab, who was in a chariot, back to Jezreel and won—on foot (vv. 45–46)! You'd think Elijah would have been standing on a mountain of unshakable faith. But when he heard Jezebel's threat, "he was afraid and arose and ran for his life and came to Beersheba, which belongs to Judah, and left his servant there" (v. 3).[4]

Beersheba was about a hundred miles south of Jezreel, but that still wasn't far enough away from wicked Jezebel. So Elijah went even farther into the wilderness, and there he sat, all alone, under a juniper tree.

And he prayed to die (v. 4).

An Interlude: Analysis of Disillusionment

As we look at this poor soul with his head buried between his knees, longing for death's relief, we ache with him. Why? Because we have visited that same juniper, and maybe we, too, have yearned for heaven's release. So for a few moments, let's examine five factors that led to his depression, factors that sometimes surface in our lives as well.

First: *Elijah was not thinking realistically or clearly.* When threatened by Jezebel, Elijah didn't consider the source—Jezebel was God's enemy, an idol worshiper, and had no authority over God's elect. Nor did Elijah question the threat itself. Could it have been

---

4. Before this incident, Elijah had been eluding Jezebel, who had previously issued a decree to kill all the prophets of the Lord (see 18:3–15).

just a bluff? Where was God's presence in all of this? And most importantly, Elijah neglected to immediately call upon the Lord. Like us in stressful situations, he forgot to stop and pray. Had he fallen on his knees before hightailing it south, he might have recaptured his sense of perspective in this situation.

Second: *Elijah had separated himself from strengthening relationships.* Elijah kept his servant with him until Beersheba, but he went into the wilderness alone. Often, a disillusioned person wants to escape from relationships. But depression feeds on loneliness, for we are most susceptible to depression's damaging effects when we are isolated from the strength that friendships can bring (see Eccles. 4:9–12).

Third: *Elijah had just come off a great victory.* Depression frequently comes on the heels of a great triumph. For Elijah, this extremely vulnerable time took him off guard, and he got caught in a Monday-morning quagmire.

Fourth: *Elijah was physically exhausted and emotionally spent.* During the last few years, Elijah's ministry had been full-speed ahead. And in the last few days, he had been riding the redline without any rest. When the adrenaline dried up, he was left physically and emotionally burned out. When that happens, our minds can play tricks on us, exaggerating tame trials into vicious nightmares.

Fifth: *Elijah had fallen into the grasp of the beast Self-pity.* "O Lord, take my life, for I am not better than my fathers" (1 Kings 19:4). But whoever said Elijah had to be better than his fathers? His self-standard was perfection, so when he came up short, he felt sorry for himself. Elijah also lamented several times that no one else was faithful to the Lord and that he was "all alone" (see 18:22; 19:10, 14). In reality, God still had thousands of believers who were faithful to Him (v. 18), but Elijah, in his self-pity, wanted to legitimize his depression by complaining that he was all alone. Poor me!

At this point, many would be tempted to take the General Patton approach and slap some sense into this blubbering prophet. But the Lord has a different method.

The Response of the Lord

Instead of rebuking him, commanding him to get busy, loading guilt on him, or shaming his tender emotions, the Lord gently picks Elijah up and sets him on his feet again.

He Allowed Him Rest and Refreshment

The Lord knows that His man needs rest and nourishment, so, through a miraculous provision, God ministers to Elijah's physical needs.

And he lay down and slept under a juniper tree; and behold, there was an angel touching him, and he said to him, "Arise, eat." Then he looked and behold, there was at his head a bread cake baked on hot stones, and a jar of water. So he ate and drank and lay down again. (vv. 5–6)

Like a loving nursemaid, the angel of the Lord tends to Elijah. It is beautiful to see how our God, who needs neither sleep nor nourishment, understands the physical needs of people. J. Oswald Sanders once wrote, "Going to bed early and a change of diet will settle many a case of depression." And French philosopher Le Maistre went even further when he said, "I have so much to do that I must go to bed"![5] God never expects us to be superhuman, so we should never feel negligent when we rest and play and laugh.

He Communicated Wisely with Elijah

Gently, tenderly, and with great insight, God speaks to Elijah: "Arise, eat, because the journey is too great for you" (v. 7b). Elijah responds by traveling forty days to Mount Horeb[6] in the strength of the food God had given him (v. 8). And there the Lord speaks to him again.

Then he came there to a cave, and lodged there; and behold, the word of the Lord came to him, and He said to him, "What are you doing here, Elijah?" (v. 9)

Rather than issuing a command or rebuke, God simply asks him a question. And the communication lines are open. Elijah repeats his miserable lamentation about being all alone (v. 10); but instead of contradicting him, God uses a different strategy.

So He said, "Go forth, and stand on the mountain before the Lord." And behold, the Lord was passing by! And a great and strong wind was rending the mountains and breaking in pieces the rocks before the Lord; but the Lord was not in the wind. And

5. J. Oswald Sanders, *A Spiritual Clinic* (Chicago, Ill.: Moody Press, 1958), p. 40.

6. Mount Horeb is also known as Mount Sinai and has always been a significant meeting place for God and His people (see Exod. 3, 19–20).

after the wind an earthquake, but the Lord was not in the earthquake. And after the earthquake a fire, but the Lord was not in the fire; and after the fire a sound of a gentle blowing. And it came about when Elijah heard it, that he wrapped his face in his mantle, and went out and stood in the entrance of the cave. (vv. 11–13a)

God has no lecture for Elijah, only an object lesson. When we are depressed, feeling alone and unloved, God comes to us in a "gentle blowing"—not in noise and commotion. So we should look for Him in the quietness of a starry sky or the stillness of a mountain meadow. Communion with God is best in our times of quiet.

But Elijah is still not through complaining: "And I alone am left; and they seek my life, to take it away" (v. 14b). And God again gently corrects without criticism or impatience. "Yet I will leave 7,000 in Israel, all the knees that have not bowed to Baal and every mouth that has not kissed him." (v. 18)

He Gave Him a Close, Personal Friend

Foremost among those seven thousand is one man whom God chose to be Elijah's kindred spirit—Elisha.

So he departed from there and found Elisha the son of Shaphat, while he was plowing with twelve pairs of oxen before him, and he with the twelfth. And Elijah passed over to him and threw his mantle on him. (v. 19)

After saying good-bye to his parents, Elisha commits himself to the Lord's service. And the story concludes, "He arose and followed Elijah and ministered to him" (vv. 20–21).

This story ends happily with the two prophets shouldering the ministry together. Elijah has found his needed rest, companionship, and communion with the Lord; and later, this prophet who prayed to die even escapes death when God takes him to heaven by way of a whirlwind and a chariot of fire (2 Kings 2:11).

A Final Thought

In John Bunyan's The Pilgrim's Progress, the main character, Christian, falls like Elijah into the Slough of Despond. Even with his cumbersome burden, Christian does not lose all hope; but he still cannot manage his way out of the mire. Finally, Help comes and assists him out of the pit. When Christian asks his new friend why this slough is here for travelers to stumble into, Help responds, "This miry slough is such a place as cannot be mended."[7]

Pits of despair that "cannot be mended" are likewise strewn throughout our lives. But the Lord is our Help, who with a firm but gentle hand can reach down and draw us out. And when our struggle is over, we can turn back and bend down to give a hand to another helpless pilgrim sinking in the miry Slough of Despond.

 Living Insights STUDY ONE

Al Capp had a terrific way of illustrating what it feels like to be depressed in the old cartoon strip *Li'l Abner.* Wherever the jinxed character Joe went, Al always drew a black rain cloud hanging just above his head. That is a perfect picture of depression—always gloomy, always dark, and always lonely. Everyone else seems to be romping in the sunshine, but for people like ol' Joe, the blues are ever present.

If God were drawing a cartoon of you right now, would He put a rain cloud above your head too? What kind would it be?

☐ A small cloud that comes and goes with the natural disappointments of life.

☐ A dreary, pervasive, fog-like cloud that creeps into every nook and cranny.

☐ A crashing thunderhead that bears down on you, leaving you fearful that you are unable to function.

Thankfully, God has designed us with the ability to process our feelings of loss and sadness, to grieve, and then to recover. This process works best when we have routinely shored up our foundation of emotional and physical well-being. Ask yourself the following questions, and pray for God's strength to build up the areas of your life that are vulnerable to out-of-control depression.

7. John Bunyan, *The Pilgrim's Progress* (Old Tappan, N.J.: Fleming H. Revell Co., n.d.), p. 8.

- When I experience a loss, on what should I focus my thoughts so that I can perceive the situation clearly?

  _____

  _____

  _____

- In what ways can my friendships be a strength to me when I'm discouraged?

  _____

  _____

  _____

- How can I refresh myself after an exhausting accomplishment in order to avoid depression?

  _____

  _____

  _____

- How do I rate my physical shape? What would help me become more physically energized?

  _____

  _____

  _____

- How have my thoughts about myself been affecting my attitude? In what ways can I be more positive and confident?

  _____

  _____

  _____

These five factors are vital in preventing depression. But what about the person who is already depressed? How can you be a support to that person? The answer to that question is the focus of Study Two.

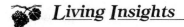

The woman in the introduction of today's lesson is an example of someone with severe depression. She experienced a persistent gloominess that affected her ability to function and to relate to others. She was suspicious of her friends, even if they tried encouraging her. She was unable to sleep at night, and her health had declined. Battling feelings of self-hatred, she even attempted hurting herself. She was on a dark, downward staircase, and with each step, she descended deeper and deeper into her own private agony.

Words of advice, such as "You should try reading your Bible" or "Think of all your blessings" or "God is disciplining you, and you need to confess your sin," are not a soothing balm to a person in depression. In fact, those words can even force him or her into deeper guilt and frustration. Instead, we need to follow the Lord's example as He compassionately counseled Elijah.

First, He took care of Elijah's physical needs. Many times, severe depression is caused by a chemical imbalance in the body or other physical problems. If you have a friend in deep depression, that person may need to see a doctor. What doctors in your community understand depression and can offer advice? And how can you help provide your friend an opportunity for rest and refreshment?

_____

_____

_____

Also, the Lord communicated gently with Elijah. What can you do or say to that person to express your unconditional acceptance and love? Write down a list of ideas.

_____

_____

_____

Then, by giving him Elisha, the Lord met Elijah's need for friendship. Listening attentively and relying on the Lord for wisdom will help you perceive your friend's real need. That need usually results from a loss in life, like the loss of respect or the loss of feeling loved. What loss do you think sparked your friend's depression? How can you help that person accept the loss?[8]

Their loss: _____

_____

How you can help them accept their loss: _____

_____

_____

_____

_____

Ministering to the depressed is a long-term commitment. Are your resources becoming exhausted? The same God who refused to give up on Elijah offeres the love and endurance you need today.

8. For further information on the subject of depression, we recommend *Happiness Is a Choice*, by Frank Minirth and Paul Meier; *Counseling the Depressed*, by Archibald Hart; and *Depression Hits Every Family*, by Grace Ketterman. Also the Insight for Living Counseling Department is available to answer any questions you may have. To contact one of the counselors, write to P.O. Box 69000, Anaheim, CA 92817-0900.

Chapter 6

THE OFFICER WHOSE LEPROSY WAS CLEANSED

2 Kings 5:1–14

The words of the prophet Isaiah paint a vivid backdrop, providing a spiritual context for today's unfolding drama.

> Seek the Lord while He may be found;
> Call upon Him while He is near.
> Let the wicked forsake his way,
> And the unrighteous man his thoughts;
> And let him return to the Lord,
> And He will have compassion on him;
> And to our God,
> For He will abundantly pardon.
> "For My thoughts are not your thoughts,
> Neither are your ways My ways," declares the Lord.
> "For as the heavens are higher than the earth,
> So are My ways higher than your ways,
> And My thoughts than your thoughts."
> (Is. 55:6–9)

These words, familiar to and well-loved by most of us, are addressed to those who do not yet know the Lord. In verses 6–7, the prophet invites them to seek God, but he also issues an implicit warning that those who come must abandon their wicked way of life as well as their unrighteous thoughts. If they will, God promises two things: He will have compassion on them and He will pardon them.

Then, in the rest of the passage (vv. 8–9), God Himself clarifies that there is a surprise factor in coming to Him. The surprise is that He thinks differently than we do, that His ways are beyond predicting, and that His plan for our lives is much higher than our own.

Like a puzzle with a missing piece, His infinite thoughts and ways and plans are intriguing, mystifying, and sometimes frustrating to our finite minds.

One person who wrestled with the puzzling methods of God was an unbeliever named Naaman (2 Kings 5:1). To him, God's path followed no pattern and didn't make sense at all. Will he follow it anyway, seek God, and find His compassion? Or will he turn in frustration and walk away from God? Let's turn to 2 Kings and see how the truths of Isaiah 55 are enacted in this great story.

A Bit of History to Reconstruct the Setting

Naaman's story takes place at a time when God's people were in a civil war. The ten northern tribes, calling themselves Israel, had seceded from the kingdom, leaving two tribes, which took the name Judah, in the south. Tragically, none of the kings who ruled the northern tribes followed the Lord, so God had to communicate to them through His prophets—in this story, it is His prophet Elisha.

As Elijah's successor, Elisha has carried on the prophetic tradition of a faithful walk with God, which puts him out of step with his times. Into this troubled, conflict-ridden setting God places unbelieving Naaman.

The Story of a Miracle

Who is this man Naaman? And why does he come to see Elisha?

A Proud Man and His Disease

Naaman is the captain of the Syrian army, and his attributes shine like the medals on his chest. For he "was a great man with his master, and highly respected, because by him the Lord had given victory to Aram.[1] The man was also a valiant warrior" (2 Kings 5:1a).

A five-star, rough-and-ready general, Naaman commanded not only the Syrian army but also the respect of king and country. However, there was one thing he could not command—his health. For verse 1 abruptly concludes: "But he was a leper."

After facing countless enemies and prevailing, Naaman is now crossing swords with his most formidable foe—the devastating and incurable disease of leprosy. And he is losing. In God's unforeseeable plan, however, a young girl has stepped into his life and is about to send him a message of hope.

A Servant Girl and Her Counsel

Naaman would never have imagined that hope for a new life would come from a young Jewish slave girl. But then, he didn't know that God's ways are not our ways.

1. Aram and Syria are two designations for the same country, which was located north of Israel.

Now the Arameans had gone out in bands, and had
taken captive a little girl from the land of Israel; and
she waited on Naaman's wife. And she said to her
mistress, "I wish that my master were with the
prophet who is in Samaria! Then he would cure him
of his leprosy." (vv. 2–3)

Somehow the girl knew of the Lord's prophet, even though her
country did not worship the Lord at this time.[2] And she confidently
recommends him without giving Elisha's name to her mistress, who
quickly passes the information to her husband.

As he takes in his wife's words, something stirs inside. How
many useless potions and obnoxious rubs has he tried over the years?
How many so-called physicians have poked and pricked him? How
many sacrifices to his stone-faced gods has he offered? But when
he hears this news from his wife, he feels something new—a twinge
of hope in his soul.

A Desperate Search and Its Results

Naaman immediately relays the girl's words to the king, who
wholeheartedly drafts a letter to Joram,[3] the king of Israel, and
sends his captain to Samaria (vv. 4–5a). But before Naaman leaves
town, he has a few items to gather, just in case. He weighs down
his chariots with 750 pounds of silver, 150 pounds of gold, and 10
fine new suits to pay the man who heals him (v. 5b). His action
reveals the faulty reasoning of unbelievers who are starting to seek
the Lord. His first mistake is to think, *I'll buy my cleansing.*

Then, when he arrives in Israel, another action reveals a second
mistake. Thinking, *I'll get my cleansing from a man,* he goes straight
to King Joram. "This man should have some clout," Naaman reasons. So

he brought the letter to the king of Israel, saying,
"And now as this letter comes to you, behold, I have

---

2. Since Elisha had not cured a leper before Naaman (see Luke 4:27), the girl must have
assumed that he could help her master because of his other miracles (see 2 Kings 4:32–35).
Her faith in God contrasts Israel's lack of faith. See Thomas L. Constable, "2 Kings," in
The Bible Knowledge Commentary, Old Testament volume, ed. John F. Walvoord and Roy B.
Zuck (Wheaton, Ill.: SP Publications, Victor Books, 1985), p. 547.

3. Joram is also called Jehoram, the son of Ahab (see 2 Kings 3:1). He should not be
confused with Jehoram, the son of Jehoshaphat, who ruled the southern kingdom during
this same period (see 1:17).

sent Naaman my servant to you, that you may cure him of his leprosy." (v. 6)

Imagine the king of Israel's face after reading that! Israel and Syria have a long-standing history of conflict, and when suddenly the feared commander of the Syrian armies appears wanting the impossible, something sounds fishy.

And it came about when the king of Israel read the letter, that he tore his clothes and said, "Am I God, to kill and to make alive, that this man is sending word to me to cure a man of his leprosy? But consider now, and see how he is seeking a quarrel against me." (v. 7)

With wonderful irony, Israel's king, who does not worship the Lord, admits that only God could do such a miracle. Even so, he does not summon Elisha or ask God's help. But in God's remarkable way of doing things, Elisha hears about the problem and sends word to the king.

"Why have you torn your clothes? Now let him come to me, and he shall know that there is a prophet in Israel." So Naaman came with his horses and his chariots, and stood at the doorway of the house of Elisha. (vv. 8b–9)

Naaman has come to the end of his journey. Frustrated with Israel's king and tired from dusty traveling, he stands at the door . . . waiting. At home, men bow in his presence; in battle, they cower and quake. But now he is the nervous one as he waits on Elisha's doorstep, hoping to see a man he's only heard of, asking for a cure he's only dreamed about.

And Elisha sent a messenger to him, saying, "Go and wash in the Jordan seven times, and your flesh shall be restored to you and you shall be clean." (v. 10)

"What?! Isn't Elisha going to graciously receive me, pronounce some mystical blessing, wave his hands around a bit, and . . . ta da, no more leprosy?" Naaman is furious as his expectations are dashed (v. 11), which reveals his third mistake: *But this isn't the way I had in mind.*

Like all unbelievers, he must face God's "surprise factor"—that His ways are not our ways. And if Naaman will be healed, he must conquer his pride and obey God, even though he doesn't fully understand Him. But his prejudices are strong, and for a moment, his pride is winning.

> "Are not Abanah and Pharpar, the rivers of Damascus, better than all the waters of Israel? Could I not wash in them and be clean?" So he turned and went away in a rage. (v. 12)

Rather than stooping to accept the Lord's way, Naaman turns on his heels and stamps away. But, just then, he feels a tug on his sleeve.

A Humble Man and His Cleansing

Catching Naaman's attention, his servants gently confront their master. The Lord has already used a young girl and a messenger; now He is going to use a group of unknown slaves to touch Naaman's heart.

> Then his servants came near and spoke to him and said, "My father, had the prophet told you to do some great thing, would you not have done it? How much more then, when he says to you, 'Wash and be clean'?" (v. 13)

The servants' good sense appeals to Naaman, who recognizes his prideful attitude and turns his rage into repentance as he heads toward the muddy Jordan River.

> So he went down and dipped himself seven times in the Jordan, according to the word of the man of God; and his flesh was restored like the flesh of a little child, and he was clean. (v. 14)

One, two, three, four, five, six . . . seven! Naaman emerges from the water and the servants cheer with delight. This bruised and diseased soldier had finally come to the Lord with a childlike faith, so the Lord had given him a childlike flesh—new skin to match his new heart.

Lessons Learned at Naaman's Expense

Even though Naaman did not understand, even though he did not have all the pieces to the puzzle, he still believed. From his experience, we can put together four lessons about searching for God's peace and forgiveness.

First: *It's not until we accept the fact that we are diseased that we seek cleansing.* Naaman's disease was obvious; it was there for all to see. Our sin-disease is under the surface and not so obvious. It is much easier to hide behind a mask of self-righteousness. So the first step toward cleansing is to take off this mask and admit sin's presence.

Second: *It's not until we hear the truth that we discover the way to find relief.* In God's amazing plan, He uses the most unlikely people as His messengers. In Naaman's case, God used nameless servants; in our case, who knows whom God could use?

Third: *It's not until we come to the end of ourselves that we are ready to go God's way.* Our way to God may be along the paths of human reasoning, social status, or good deeds. But God says that there is only one way—His way. Following Christ means that we must abandon our own efforts, come to the end of ourselves, and humbly desire to go God's way.

Fourth: *It's not until we actually do as God requires that our cleansing takes place.* God's way may not make sense to us, because His ways are higher than ours. But if we want to know God and have peace, forgiveness, and hope beyond the grave, then we have to obey and come His way—nothing more, nothing less, nothing else. Just come.

 ## Living Insights

Like Naaman's leprosy, we have a disease called sin. Unlike leprosy, though, it is on the inside. We may deny that sin-disease and cover its symptoms, but still it exists—and it is deadly. As Larry Crabb writes,

> God could randomly select any five-minute slice from our lives and, after evaluating our thoughts, motives, and deeds during this brief period, *justly* throw us into outer darkness to wander forever alone in agony and despair. When we begin to grasp this, our excuses appear weak and our selfishness deadly.[4]

For the unbeliever, sin is terminal. For the Christian, though, we have taken a cure called grace that both has cleansed us and

---

4. Larry Crabb, *Men and Women* (Grand Rapids, Mich.: Zondervan Publishing House, 1991), p. 96.

continues to cleanse us (see Titus 2:11–14; 3:5). As a result, we can daily wash ourselves in God's grace and experience His purifying forgiveness (see 1 John 1:7–9).

But that experience is possible only when we take the first step. And that step is admitting that we are diseased. Allow the Holy Spirit to be your spiritual doctor for a moment. What sinful thoughts and actions does He see in your soul? Writing them down will help you admit them.

_____

_____

_____

Many times we recognize our habitual sins, but we overlook others that are more subtle—sins like greed, selfishness, and worry. Continue letting God's Spirit examine you. What subtle sins does He see?

_____

_____

_____

Now read Hebrews 9:11–14. What is the result of Christ's actions as our high priest?

_____

_____

_____

To experience Christ's cleansing forgiveness, we must not only admit our sin, we must also believe that because of Christ's blood we are forgiven. You can express your confession and faith through prayer. Larry Crabb has written a penetrating prayer of confession. Read it once, then again as your own, if it expresses your heart.

> Lord, at every moment of my life, regardless of the hurt I experience, your law condemns me. Your standards are right, but I cannot meet them. I am not good enough to do what you require. I am worthy of judgment. Forgiveness is my deepest need right

now and will continue to be my deepest need till I die. Because your atoning death meets that need, I can live in the freedom of forgiveness, neither obsessed with my sin nor indifferent towards it.[5]

Amen.

 Living Insights   STUDY TWO

What do a young girl, a messenger, and a group of slaves have in common? In Naaman's story, they were all unknown servants whom God used in such marvelous ways that their actions were recorded for all time in the Scriptures.

God still uses everyday folks like us for His grand purposes. And although our deeds will not be recorded in Scripture, they will be recorded in a living history—the life of someone we help.

Is there a Naaman in your life? Is there someone you know who suffers from sin's leprous effects, someone who does not know about Christ and His ability to cleanse and forgive? You may know several, but write down the name of just one person whom God is placing in your thoughts.

_____

You can fill three possible roles in that person's life. First, you can be like the little girl in your approach. What did she do to start Naaman thinking about his cleansing (2 Kings 5:3)?

_____

_____

_____

Or you can be like the messenger. What did he say to help Naaman understand how to be cleansed (v. 10)?

_____

_____

_____

5. Crabb, *Men and Women*, p. 96.

Finally, you can be like the servants. What did they say to persuade Naaman to go to the Jordan (v. 13)?

_____

_____

_____

God used each of these people uniquely in Naaman's life. He used the girl to plant the thought, the messenger to give the facts, and the slaves to gently persuade.

As you think about the person you named earlier, what is that "Naaman's" greatest need right now? Does this person need you to plant a thought about Christ, explain the facts of the gospel, or give a gentle nudge to believe and obey?

_____

_____

What specific words can you use to plant a thought, explain the gospel, or give a nudge?

_____

_____

_____

_____

_____

Had God not used these people in Naaman's life, he would never have found the release and joy of God's cleansing. Let God use you in your Naaman's life. If He can use a little girl, a messenger, and a group of servants, He can use you too.

Chapter 7

THE HELPER WHO GOT GREEDY

2 Kings 5:15–16, 19–27

Imagine being in the inner circle of the president of the United States. The feeling of power would be electrifying. But one fact would always remain obvious: the power would not be in you, but in the one you served.

What would happen, though, if a member of that inner circle became tired of serving and wanted more? If number two wanted the glory that number one possessed? Then, as in today's lesson, we would see the subtle invasion of a monster called greed.

An Analysis of Greed

Greed begins in a discontented heart, weaseling its way into the mind to affect how we think and act. To understand how greed operates, let's begin by examining its meaning.

Meaning of the Term

Essentially, greed is covetousness, an inordinate desire to acquire more and more. Greed is also the desire to have what you want now—by whatever means possible. It always thinks in excessive terms and always hurries to grab for more.

Manners of Expression

This lust for more usually shows up in four main areas of life. First, people are greedy for *money;* they will sacrifice family, friends, and health to draw that big salary and turn that higher profit. This craving for a bulging bank account then leads to another area, the greed for *things.* Money buys toys; and the one with the most toys wins . . . something—no one knows what. Third, people become greedy for *fame.* To be known and quoted, popular and influential are the goals of this greed. But there is one more kind of greed, the greed for *pleasure.* It can be any sensual pleasure—sex, food, or comforts in life. But none of these pleasures satisfy permanently; they just leave more emptiness and hunger behind.

Some people have fought these greedy temptations for years and understand their effects. But others see no such perceivable monsters in their hearts. To those, we have one word of advice: Beware! Another insidious gremlin may lurk silently in the shadows of the soul—*secret greed.*

One particular incident exposes this kind of greed, and it occurs right after the story of Naaman's cleansing.

An Account of Greed

As you recall from the previous lesson, the remarkable story unfolded like this.

Historical Background

Naaman, a leprosy victim, had come from Syria to Israel to seek healing from Elisha. But the prophet of God left Naaman standing at the doorstep, giving him a curious message to dip seven times in the Jordan River. Naaman reluctantly trekked down to the river and, on the seventh dunk, emerged clean and healed (2 Kings 5:14). Not only was Naaman's skin cleansed, so was his heart. For he said to Elisha upon returning from the Jordan,

> "Behold now, I know that there is no God in all the earth, but in Israel; so please take a present from your servant now." (v. 15b)

The pre-Jordan Naaman was arrogant and smug; the cleansed Naaman is humble, grateful, and generous. The present he offers Elisha is the 750 pounds of silver, 150 pounds of gold, and 10 fine suits he had brought from Syria (see v. 5).[1] But just as Naaman stands before Elisha as a humble servant, so Elisha stands before the Lord. And with a clear conscience, the prophet politely declines the gift.

> But he said, "As the Lord lives, before whom I stand, I will take nothing." And he urged him to take it, but he refused. (v. 16)

Despite Naaman's urgings and the glittering treasures spread in front of him, Elisha does not back down. To do so would compro-

---

1. For the conversion of shekels and talents to pounds, see Thomas L. Constable, "2 Kings," in *The Bible Knowledge Commentary*, Old Testament volume, ed. John F. Walvoord and Roy B. Zuck (Wheaton, Ill.: SP Publications, Victor Books, 1985), p. 547.

mise his calling and strike a black mark on his reputation. So, instead of taking Naaman's presents,[2] Elisha gives him a blessing, saying, "go in peace"—*shalom* (v. 19).

But standing within earshot is Gehazi, who listens with heated interest. He has been the number-two man, Elisha's supporter and servant. He has always enjoyed Elisha's reflected glory, but he harbors a secret desire—to grab some for himself.

Mental Reasoning

When Gehazi hears Naaman offer Elisha a small Fort Knox fortune, he thinks, *Now's our chance, boss, we're rich!* But while he is mentally spending his cut of the cash, he looks up and sees Naaman's camels heading north—still loaded with the treasure. *What? This can't be!* Quickly, his mind formulates a plan.

> But Gehazi, the servant of Elisha the man of God, thought, "Behold, my master has spared this Naaman the Aramean, by not receiving from his hands what he brought. As the Lord lives, I will run after him and take something from him." (v. 20)

Perhaps the greed gremlin in his soul began to feed him rationalized reasons. "Naaman just wanted to say thank you. To refuse him would be discourteous; after all, he insisted that we take it. . . . The man has millions! This is pocket change. And he did bring it all this way; no sense in his lugging it back. . . . God provides in surprising ways, doesn't He? Who would have imagined our needs being met by a Syrian? . . . Sure, Elisha can perform a miracle and God provides for him; but I have nothing. I have scrubbed his floors too long. I need the money, and I deserve it!"

All of Gehazi's rationalizations sound convincing; what's wrong with them? Well, first, the gift was offered to Elisha, not Gehazi. Furthermore, he knows his master's feelings about the money, and still he chooses to run after Naaman. It's secret greed. It's behind-the-back-while-no-one-is-looking greed, and he will not discuss his plans with Elisha. He intends to cash in on a reward his master earned; and if his plan works, no one will be the wiser.

---

2. The word for *present* in verse 15 means "blessing." Naaman wished to bless Elisha, but Elisha blessed Naaman instead.

Volitional Acts

So, after "Gehazi . . . thought" (v. 20), then "Gehazi pursued" (v. 21). Without considering God's will or concerning himself with Naaman's feelings as a new and gullible convert, Gehazi's first willful act is to *pursue the goods.*

> So Gehazi pursued Naaman. When Naaman saw one running after him, he came down from the chariot to meet him and said, "Is all well?" And he said, "All is well. My master has sent me, saying, 'Behold, just now two young men of the sons of the prophets have come to me from the hill country of Ephraim. Please give them a talent of silver and two changes of clothes.'" (vv. 21–22)

We see it happen almost in slow motion, and we want to warn Naaman. All is not well, Elisha hasn't sent anybody, and the money and clothes are for Gehazi, not for any needy prophets. *Gehazi lies,* and that is his second greedy act.

Stopping at nothing, Gehazi even uses his spiritual role to pull the wool over the Syrian's eyes. Unfortunately, Naaman believes Gehazi, and in his zeal to please the Lord, Naaman says,

> "Be pleased to take two talents." And he urged him, and bound two talents of silver in two bags with two changes of clothes, and gave them to two of his servants; and they carried them before him. (v. 23)

With two talents of silver instead of just one, the servant Gehazi is escorted home like a king. When he and Naaman's servants arrive at the hill by his home, he dismisses them, committing his third willful act of greed. Hoping Elisha won't know what he's done, *he acts deceitfully,* stashing the goods in his house (v. 24).

Finally, he must return to his master and resume his servant duties. It all went more smoothly than he had hoped. The extra silver and the little parade was a nice touch. But when he returns to Elisha's house, the prophet peers into his soul (v. 25).

"Where have you been, Gehazi?"

"Your servant went nowhere."

Consumed by his rationalizations and convinced he was right, Gehazi engages in his fourth act of greed—*he denies the truth before the one who trusted him.*

How can he lie so blatantly? Once people lie to themselves, they can lie to anyone. That's how some ministers can preach on

Sunday and be adulterous during the week. That's how top-level executives can extort money from the company and give a believable accounting to the CEO. That's how rationalization can be so effective in legitimizing secret greed.

Personal Consequences

Unlike Naaman, however, Elisha is not fooled. Instead, he penetrates Gehazi's deception with compassionate yet pointed questions:

> "Did not my heart go with you, when the man turned from his chariot to meet you? Is it a time to receive money and to receive clothes and olive groves and vineyards and sheep and oxen and male and female servants?" (v. 26)

In his careful planning, the greedy servant overlooked one crucial factor—Elisha was a seer. God allowed Elisha to see every detail of the transaction and to perceive the intentions of Gehazi, who probably planned to purchase land, animals, and servants with the loot.

Finally, Elisha pronounces a terrible judgment on his servant, a judgment full of irony.

> "Therefore, the leprosy of Naaman shall cleave to you and to your descendants forever." So he went out from his presence a leper as white as snow. (v. 27)

The leprous pagan who came in faith found forgiveness and healing, but the trusted servant of the Lord who succumbed to faithless greed was stricken with leprosy. And not only was Gehazi judged, but all his descendants as well.

An Admission of Greed

The severe discipline issued to the greedy helper in this story sets us back in our chairs because we know our own hearts. We, too, have cultivated secret greed from time to time. But God wants to teach us, through Gehazi's story, several lessons that will keep us guarded against it.

First: *Imagination allows greed to grow.* Gehazi's creative mind dreamed of wealth and power, but that dream soon turned into a nightmare. Our imaginations, if unchecked, may also spin fantasies of fame and fortune. So we must remember to focus on what is godly and appropriate in order to stop greed early (see Rom. 13:14).

Second: *Rationalization encourages greed to surface.* Imaginations quickly turn into rationalizations, which are convincing reasons to believe what is untrue. They say: stealing is OK, lying is all right, and the end justifies the means. That kind of thinking can convince people to leave their families or encourage an employee to cover the truth if lying will aid advancement. Eventually, under rationalization's guise, greed surfaces.

Third: *Deception gives greed courage to persist.* For greedy behavior to continue, it requires secrecy. So we lie to ourselves, which enables us to lie to others—even those closest to us.

Fourth: *Confession brings greed to a necessary and abrupt halt.* Ultimately, though, no amount of lying can cover up the truth. Greed is ugly no matter how much spiritual makeup we apply. It is naked avarice, and confession is the only remedy. Admitting our sin of greed means facing our true, sinful natures. But the good news is, in doing this we will find the power of Jesus Christ to stop greed in its tracks and to allow us to walk freely with a clear conscience.

Gehazi's skin became a lifelong reminder of his secret greed. And for those like Gehazi, who are in an inner circle and share the limelight with someone well known, the temptation to grab for unearned glory and privilege can be especially overwhelming. Take out the mirror of God's Word and examine your motives. If secret greed stalks silently in your heart, admit it, and bring that monster to the Lord. The One who crushed greed at the Cross can conquer it in your heart as well.

 Living Insights

A celebrity usually has one. A star athlete has one too. A politician definitely has one, and even a pastor has one. What could these diverse people have in common? They all have an inner circle.

An inner circle is a group of friends who surround a popular person and enjoy many of the benefits that person has earned. Gehazi was a part of Elisha's inner circle; he may have even been Elisha's closest companion. But he wanted more privileges than he had, and greed took root in his soul.

Are you a part of an inner circle? It may surround your pastor, an influential person at work, a leader in your community or church, or just a well-liked person. If so, describe the group and who its center is.

_____

_____

In inner circles, greed can have many voices. It can use the voice of power, convincing you to take over. It can use the voice of jealousy, persuading you to monopolize friendships. Have you ever heard greed's subtle voice? What was it telling you?

_____

_____

Have you obeyed greed's voice and said or done something that you now realize was motivated by that nasty gremlin? What did you say or do?

_____

_____

As we noted in the lesson, confession brings greed to a necessary and abrupt halt. Do you need to apologize to someone? Is there some action you should take to restore damaged feelings? Don't let secret greed consume you or your cherished friendships. Take care of it today.

 ## Living Insights   STUDY TWO

Greed has many expressions. One is the look on a teenager's face when she sees her best friend's closet packed with new clothes. Another is the longing gaze the middle-aged dad gives his neighbor's new Porsche. It's the look executives have when they see their chance to take someone's place in the boss's inner circle. And its the dreamy ponder on a tired mom's face when she flips on *Lifestyles of the Rich and Famous*.

Essentially, greed has a hungry look. It says, "I'm not satisfied with what I own, what I control, or whom I influence. I'm hungry for more." Reflect on what kind of looks you've been giving lately. Concerning money, things, fame, and pleasure, rate yourself on a scale of one to five, with one being "peaceful contentment" and five being "longing hunger."

How do I look when thoughts of making more money cross my mind?

1   2   3   4   5

When TV ads tempt me to acquire more things?

1   2   3   4   5

When opportunities arise that may make me more well known?

1   2   3   4   5

When I'm tempted to pursue more pleasure?

1   2   3   4   5

If you see more longing hunger than peaceful contentment, there is something you need to know about such hunger: it is never satisfied. George MacDonald writes, "The heart of man cannot hoard. His brain or his hand may gather into its box and hoard, but the moment the thing has passed into the box, the heart has lost it and is hungry again."[3]

If money, things, fame, or pleasure do not satisfy, then what will? Read Philippians 4:11–13.

Paul says that he has learned contentment. What circumstances were his teachers (vv. 11–12)?

_____

_____

To what does "all things" refer (v. 13), and how do you think Christ can provide the strength for those things?

_____

_____

Christ satisfies our hunger. As MacDonald says, "If a man would *have*, it is the Giver he must have."[4] So, when you sense greed's wondering look in your eye, admit your hunger pangs. And turn your face toward Christ who, whether in riches or want, will always satisfy.

3. George MacDonald, in *George MacDonald: An Anthology*, ed. C. S. Lewis (New York, N.Y.: Macmillan Publishing Co., 1974), p. 119.

4. MacDonald, *George MacDonald: An Anthology*, p. 119.

Chapter 8

THE SERVANT WHO SAW THE INVISIBLE

2 Kings 6:8–20

"The Carasoyn" is a delightful fairy tale told by the nineteenth-century writer George MacDonald. In the story, a young boy must rescue a girl whom the fairies have captured and reduced to their tiny size. He sets out to find help from an old woman he had once met when lost in the woods. Searching for hours in vain, he realizes that he is lost again. And suddenly, there before his eyes is the old woman's house. MacDonald then teaches us a wise lesson through the boy's words:

> "It seems the way to find some things is to lose yourself," said he to himself.[1]

Likewise, it is at those times in our Christian walk when we are lost in fear, worry, or grief that God appears out of nowhere. In our most desperate hour, God discloses Himself; and we see Him and His glory in a new and comforting way. As Webster's dictionary says, God's action at such a time is "an extraordinary event manifesting divine intervention in human affairs"[2]—a miracle.

This kind of "extraordinary event" happened long ago to the prophet Elisha and his servant when they were surrounded by enemy forces. Certain death crept so close that they could feel its icy breath. But Elisha remained calm, even though his servant shivered in fear. For the man of God could see what his servant couldn't, and that made all the difference.

Some Historical Background to the Story

As we mentioned in a previous chapter, Elisha's homeland shook from the rumblings of prolonged civil war. Just as the United States did during the American Civil War, the Israelite nation had split

---

1. George MacDonald, "The Carasoyn," *The Gifts of the Child Christ* (Grand Rapids, Mich.: William B. Eerdmans Publishing Co., 1973), vol. 2, p. 83.

2. *Webster's Ninth New Collegiate Dictionary*, see "miracle."

into north and south, each side having a capital and a head of state. Israel, the northern territory, had nineteen kings parade across its two-hundred-year stage of history. And all nineteen worshiped other gods, rebelling against the Lord.

Still, God loved His people, so He anointed prophets like Elijah, Jonah, Hosea, Amos, and Elisha through whom he communicated. Men of iron-willed determination, they were empowered by God to influence Israel in extraordinary ways. But being a prophet in those days was dangerous business. It had its risks, and Elisha knew them well. One such risk came early one morning when his servant awoke to the sound of enemy chariots on every side.

The Main Plot of the Story

Who had sent an army to surround Elisha's city? Why would anyone do this? And what was Elisha going to do? Let's turn to 2 Kings 6 to discover the answers.

The Characters

Our story's cast of characters begins with Ben-hadad, the king of Syria (vv. 8a, 24). He is Israel's enemy and a particular thorn in the flesh to Jehoram, the king of Israel (vv. 9–10).[3] Caught in the middle of this conflict of kings is Elisha, "the man of God" (v. 9). And, as in many of the stories in 2 Kings, two servants also play vital roles—Ben-hadad has an unnamed servant and so does Elisha.[4]

The Situation

Just like a disagreeable neighbor, Syria had been testing Israel along their shared border. Ben-hadad had strategized his encroachments by moving secretly from place to place. But each time he did so, Jehoram reinforced the new areas to which Ben-hadad had moved. How did Israel's king know where the next attack would come from? A certain person intercepted Ben-hadad's plans and anticipated his every move. That spy was Elisha, who supernaturally received the valuable military information from the Lord (vv. 9–10).

---

3. This son of Ahab and Jezebel is also known as Joram, and his reign is recorded from 1:17 to 9:24 (see also 3:1; 8:16, 25, 28; 9:14–23).

4. If this incident followed chronologically the one in which Gehazi contracted Naaman's leprosy, then Elisha's servant was probably not Gehazi but another "attendant of the man of God" (see v. 15; 5:27).

In his tent, Ben-hadad flailed his arms in rage. One thwarted surprise attack is understandable, two is coincidence. But three, four, five attacks anticipated? There must be a leak! "Will you tell me," screamed the frustrated commander, "which of us is for the king of Israel?" (v. 11b).

Enter the unknown Syrian servant who is wiser than kings.

> And one of his servants said, "No, my lord, O king; but Elisha, the prophet who is in Israel, tells the king of Israel the words that you speak in your bed-room." (v. 12)

How did Ben-hadad's servant know about Elisha? Could he have been acquainted with Naaman, the leprous Syrian commander whom Elisha's God had healed? Did he believe in the Lord too? We are not told. But we do know that he had remarkable insight to perceive Elisha's hot line to the Lord—the God who sees all and hears all, even secret strategies whispered in a king's bedchamber.

So Ben-hadad determines to "take"[5] the prophet-spy (v. 13), and he sends a "great army" to Dothan where Elisha and his attendant are living. Under the cover of darkness, the Syrians slip through the Israelite defenses and quietly surround the sleeping city (v. 14).

The Reaction

The next morning, Elisha's servant stirs early to prepare for the day. But he is not prepared for what he sees outside the city gate. Gleaming shields and swords reflect the morning sun, and rows of chariots, archers, and war horses form menacing phalanxes are on all sides. Bug-eyed and trembling, he runs to Elisha: "Alas, my master! What shall we do?" (v. 15b).

His reaction resulted from his limited vision. He saw the numbers of soldiers and their cruel weapons, and he panicked. "How can we escape? How can we survive? We are trapped!"

Elisha, on the other hand, reacts calmly: "Do not fear" (v. 16a). He is confident during the crisis, but not because he knows of an escape tunnel or has an ingenious defense planned. He is cool and courageous because he can see something no one else sees—the invisible. And he reassures his servant that "those who are with us are more than those who are with them" (v. 16b).

---

5. Ben-hadad ordered that Elisha be brought to him, possibly for the purpose of execution (see "send and bring" in 1 Sam. 20:31).

Who are "those with us"? And who are "those with them"? Elisha sees the spiritual forces of God and knows they can overpower the forces of darkness that are with the Syrians. But his poor servant is still perplexed and afraid, so Elisha has compassion on him and asks the Lord to open his eyes to the world of the supernatural.

> Then Elisha prayed and said, "O Lord, I pray, open his eyes, that he may see." And the Lord opened the servant's eyes, and he saw; and behold, the mountain was full of horses and chariots of fire all around Elisha. (v. 17)

Dothan is surrounded by mighty angelic forces, a special detachment of fiery chariots sent to guard Elisha. Where he once saw empty air, Elisha's servant sees heaven's warriors ready to do battle.

If only we could see God's armies too! Such a vision would impress us with God's overwhelming power like it did Elisha's servant. But we do not necessarily need to see to know. As Donald Barnhouse wrote,

> Ordinarily the human eye cannot see the spiritual forces that are arrayed in the invisible realm. The eye of faith can look into the Word of God and know the truth of the power of the Lord we serve, and can be sure that nothing can ever touch us unless it has passed through the will of God. We can be sure that though there may be wisdom on the other side, omniscience is on our side alone. We may be sure that though we find an enemy to be potent, we can find that our God alone is omnipotent.[6]

The Result

For a time, Elisha's servant just stands there, absorbing the glory of God's angelic beings. Then Elisha prays again, this time for God to blind the eyes of the Syrians who were marching down the hill toward the city (v. 18).[7] God answers his prayer, and Elisha puts the rest of his plan in action.

---

6. Donald Grey Barnhouse, *The Invisible War* (Grand Rapids, Mich.: Zondervan Publishing House, 1965), p. 134.

7. This blindness is probably not literal but a "lack of recognition." See *The Wycliffe Bible Commentary*, ed. Charles F. Pfeiffer and Everett F. Harrison (Chicago, Ill.: Moody Press, 1962), p. 346.

Then Elisha said to them, "This is not the way, nor is this the city; follow me and I will bring you to the man whom you seek." And he brought them to Samaria.

And it came about when they had come into Samaria, that Elisha said, "O Lord, open the eyes of these men, that they may see." So the Lord opened their eyes, and they saw; and behold, they were in the midst of Samaria. (vv. 19–20)

The gates slam shut, their eyes are opened, and now they are the ones surrounded. God has a terrific sense of irony!

That day the Lord taught Israel and Syria an unforgettable lesson: Nations may have intimidating armies, and kings may give orders and make grandiose plans, but God is the One in control. So, as Elisha said, we have no cause to fear.

Years earlier, King David also expressed that fearless faith in God's sovereignty and power.

I sought the Lord, and He answered me,
And delivered me from all my fears. . . .
This poor man cried and the Lord heard him;
And saved him out of all his troubles.
The angel of the Lord encamps around those who
fear Him,
And rescues them.
(Ps. 34:4, 6–7; see also Ps. 91)

Tirelessly commanding His forces to fight the enemy on our behalf, God performs countless miracles every day, as He guards us against visible and invisible dangers. God's protecting power is truly astounding!

A Few Lessons from the Story

From this remarkable story several flags of confidence can be planted in our hearts to help us face fearful situations.

First: *Intimidating odds and visible obstacles mean nothing to the righteous.* Overcoming the obstacles we encounter may seem like trying to light a match in a windstorm. But we must stop focusing on the odds and the obstacles and start remembering that He who is with us is greater than he who is with them.

69

Second: *Those on the Lord's side are never outnumbered.* Those who resist the truth may appear to be in the majority, but that is never really the case—not when we consider the unseen hosts.

Third: *When God wins, it's always a landslide victory.* He never squeaks by. He never wins in the final minutes with a desperate downfield pass. His victory is sure, and it always leaves no doubt that He is in control.

"Those who are with us," Elisha said, "are more than those who are with them" (2 Kings 6:16). Since that is true, barriers can be broken and lives can be changed. Since that is true, wrongs can be righted and evil governments can fall. Since that is true, fears can be calmed and prayers will return answered.

Since that is true, miracles can happen.

 ## *Living Insights*

The boy prince was terrified of the sea. So the adults decided to cure him of his fear by picking him up and tossing him into the water. He struggled and sputtered, finally making his way back to dry land. Screaming and crying, he ran away from the waves as fast as he could. Finally caught and soothed, he was asked why he was so afraid of the sea. He could stand near soldiers and their booming cannons and not flinch; why did water scare him so? The young ruler thought for a moment and then replied, "Because I'm in command of the soldiers, but I'm not in command of the sea."[8]

Like the prince, we also have seas of fear—things we cannot command or control. We cannot control the thoughts of others, so we fear their opinions of us. We cannot control our futures, so we fear tomorrow. What are the particular seas in which you are struggling?

_____

_____

_____

_____

8. *The Little, Brown Book of Anecdotes*, ed. Clifton Fadiman (Boston, Mass.: Little, Brown and Co., 1985), p. 422.

When Elisha was thrown into a situation he could not control, he still had peace because he knew Someone who could. How well do you know that Someone? If you would have peace supplant your fears, you need to get acquainted with the character and power of God. And one of the best ways to do this is through His Word. So read the following verses, and write how God's promises calm a fear you listed above.

Psalm 27:1–3 _____

_____

Jeremiah 32:17 _____

_____

Philippians 4:19 _____

_____

Hebrews 13:5–6 _____

_____

The more you know God, the more you will trust Him. And the more you trust God, the less fear will control you. Helen Keller expressed this thought well when she commented on her plane trip around the world: "It's wonderful to climb the liquid mountains of the sky. Behind me and before me is God and I have no fears."[9]

Behind you and before you is God. You can trust Him, whatever your fears.

 Living Insights STUDY TWO

Elisha experienced God behind and before him in a supernatural way, for God stationed His heavenly soldiers around him, an army that far surpassed the enemy's strength.

But Elisha was a special case, wasn't he? God doesn't surround me with celestial armies . . . does He?

9. Helen Keller, in *Simpson's Contemporary Quotations*, comp. James B. Simpson (Boston, Mass.: Houghton Mifflin Co., 1988), p. 149.

Scripture tells us that God and His armies *do* fight for us in the heavenly realms, protecting us physically (Ps. 34:7) and spiritually (1 John 5:18). In fact, the Lord goes beyond merely surrounding us. He indwells us as well.

As you look up the following verses, write down God's promises of power and protection.

Romans 8:10–11, 31–39 _____

_____

_____

_____

2 Corinthians 10:3–4 _____

_____

1 John 4:4 _____

_____

These verses tell us that in fearful situations we have a far greater foundation for confidence than even Elisha experienced. For Christ Himself is within us, protecting us and fighting for us. We may not be able to see Him at work, but He is there just the same.

But someday we *will* see the invisible. And, like Elisha's servant, our eyes will be opened, and we will stand in the presence of angels, blinking in the light of God's glory. And we will realize that He was there all along.

Chapter 9

THE COMMISSIONER
WHO SLEPT
WITH LIONS

Daniel 6

But I didn't do it!" The words are barely out of the boy's mouth
when his father gives him a verbal slap—
"You're lying!"

"But . . . I . . . ," stutters the boy between tears.

"Go to your room and don't come out 'til you're ready to tell
the truth."

"Why don't you believe me?" the boy says, searching for understanding in his father's face but seeing only hardness.

The father speaks no more, just raises his arm and points. Defeated, the boy turns and goes to his room, where he sees a plastic
airplane on the floor. Not thinking, he kicks the innocent toy,
breaking it into a hundred pieces.

Have you ever been unjustly accused? It makes you feel like the
boy—*and* the toy airplane—doesn't it? Kicked without cause, judged
guilty when innocent, cited for a wrong when you did right.

Long ago, that happened to an honest and noble Jew named
Daniel. However, when he suffered for doing right, he wasn't sent to
his room as punishment, he was sent to the den . . . the lions' den.

Comparative Scriptures That Make the Story Live

As a young man, Daniel had been captured and taken to a
foreign land to serve a pagan king. Many years passed, and now, in
the twilight of his life, he must face his greatest test. Yet through
the ordeal Daniel exhibits a remarkable servant spirit and an amazing endurance of unfair treatment, giving us a living example of
what to do when one suffers wrong for doing right.

Interestingly, Daniel's story closely follows the principles on
unjust suffering written by the apostle Peter. The following chart
compares 1 Peter 2 and Daniel 6, so that you can clearly see God's
principles in action in Daniel's life.

Peter's Principles (1 Peter 2)	Daniel's Realities (Daniel 6)
Submit to rulers, who bring punishment or praise. (vv. 13–14)	Daniel serves King Darius with an "extraordinary spirit" and is elevated above his peers. (vv. 1–3)
Fulfill God's will through silencing wickedness by doing right. (v. 15)	Daniel's enemies try to find some wrong in him but are silenced by his integrity. (v. 4)
Respectfully submit to good and bad masters alike, for bearing injustice for con-science' sake finds favor with God. (vv. 18–19)	Daniel suffers unjustly for continuing to worship God despite the king's decree against it. (vv. 5–10)
Patiently enduring suffering after you've done what is right finds favor with God. (v. 20)	Daniel allows himself to be cast into the lions' den. God shuts the lions' mouths, pun-ishes Daniel's enemies, and receives glory from Darius' new edict endorsing worship. (vv. 11–28)

From the beginning, Daniel's integrity was his strength. In fact, Daniel's character was so inculpable that his enemies had to create a law against praying to God in order to accuse him of anything. Yet despite the unfair decree, Daniel continued to pray as always, even giving thanks to God (Dan. 6:10). He knew that breaking the law in this way would lead him straight to the lions' den. But he prayed anyway, and God was pleased.

We also may feel the cold winds of suffering for the sake of right. A boss, coworker, or even a friend may plot against us because of our stand for truth. And when the dark clouds of persecution gather, it may seem that what James Russell Lowell penned over a century ago is true:

> Truth forever on the scaffold, Wrong forever on the throne. —[1]

1. James Russell Lowell, as quoted in Bartlett's Familiar Quotations, 15th ed., rev. and enl., ed. Emily Morison Beck (Boston, Mass.: Little, Brown and Co., 1980), p. 567.

But it is important to remember that showing patience while suffering for Christ finds favor with the Lord. And as Lowell notes, despite the jumble of right and wrong:

> Yet that scaffold sways the future, and, behind the dim unknown,
> Standeth God within the shadow, keeping watch above his own.[2]

Intriguing Plot That Makes the Story Memorable

God does watch His own, and what He saw when Daniel's faith was under fire pleased Him—for his faith was consistent with his godly reputation.

Reputation of the Prophet Daniel

Daniel's reputation as a worshiper of God and as a man of integrity was a rebuke to those with lower standards. His life threatened and embarrassed them, so they retaliated. But when the accusations started flying, God honored Daniel's consistency and patient endurance.

Accusation of Daniel's Peers

Daniel's antagonists stake him out, watching and waiting. Through his window, they see him praying. And as if in a scene from a police show, they knock down his door and storm the room. "Freeze! Drop your prayer book and put your hands where we can see 'em."

With cocky grins, they cuff him and drag him before the king. And, snickering, they remind Darius of his edict, especially enjoying the part about the lions' den (Dan. 6:11–12).

Then they make their accusation:

> "Daniel, who is one of the exiles from Judah, pays no attention to you, O king, or to the injunction which you signed, but keeps making his petition three times a day." (v. 13)

Notice their prejudice against Daniel, the Jew. Rather than call him by his title of commissioner, they describe him as "one of the exiles from Judah." Also, notice how they exaggerate the truth,

---

2. Lowell, *Bartlett's Familiar Quotations*, p. 567.

75

saying "Daniel . . . pays no attention to you, O king." They knew of the tight bond between Darius and Daniel, so they tried to strain that relationship in their accusations.

We can learn some valuable lessons here for those times when we are accusing others of wrong. First, take care that you aren't guided by your prejudices. Prejudice has no place in confrontation. And second, stay with the facts. Don't exaggerate and paint a bleaker picture than what's really there. If you'll take to heart this negative example of the satraps and commissioners, you will learn to value fairness and practice it that much more.

And how does the king react to these accusations? He knows the law, but before him stands his beloved friend who is now a lawbreaker. Kill the law, or kill his friend. What a dilemma!

Reaction of King Darius

Darius probably wishes he could be anywhere but on his throne, having to decide Daniel's fate. God is working in his heart, though, as we see in the different ways he reacts to this situation.

First, Darius reacts *to himself*, as he realizes his mistake.

> As soon as the king heard this statement, he was deeply distressed and set his mind on delivering Daniel; and even until sunset he kept exerting himself to rescue him. (v. 14)

What motivated the king to agonize over this case? Apparently, Darius was an honest man, though not a believer, and he wanted to do the right thing. Also, Daniel was his friend. In spite of their different religious beliefs, the two men found an uncommon closeness and loyalty to one another. So, in an effort to save Daniel, King Darius paces. And thinks. And wrestles in his mind for hours. There must be a loophole, there must!

But by day's end, Darius' searching yields nothing; and the accusers say impatiently, "Recognize, O king, that it is a law of the Medes and Persians that no injunction or statute which the king establishes may be changed" (v. 15).

Then the cornered king reacts *to Daniel*. With his head hanging low, the king slowly pronounces the orders: "Throw him to the lions." But before Darius turns away, he speaks to his friend.

> "Your God whom you constantly serve will Himself deliver you." (v. 16b)

For a non-believer, Darius has remarkable faith in God! Daniel exhibits iron trust too, for without panic, he quietly allows the guards to toss him into the pit.[3] And they close the opening with a stone that is sealed by the king and his nobles (v. 17). Now all they can do is wait.

> Then the king went off to his palace and spent the night fasting, and no entertainment was brought before him; and his sleep fled from him. (v. 18)

The king debates inwardly all night. Reason says, "Daniel is a dead man"; hope says, "Daniel's God can save him." And his troubled heart asks, "What is happening in that pit?"

> Then the king arose with the dawn, at the break of day, and went in haste to the lions' den. And when he had come near the den to Daniel, he cried out with a troubled voice. The king spoke and said to Daniel, "Daniel, servant of the living God, has your God, whom you constantly serve, been able to deliver you from the lions?" Then Daniel spoke to the king, "O king, live forever! My God sent His angel and shut the lions' mouths, and they have not harmed me, inasmuch as I was found innocent before Him; and also toward you, O king, I have committed no crime." (vv. 19–22)

While Darius tossed and turned in bed, Daniel had slept peacefully with the lions. Amazing! For one night, God had removed the lions' killer instinct, and the next morning Daniel stands next to the disarmed beasts, chatting with the king. Unharmed, Daniel is finally lifted from the den (v. 23).

Now it is time for King Darius to react *to Daniel's accusers*. He gives orders to round them up, and with an ironic twist, he sentences those who had been slanderously "eating up"[4] Daniel to be

---

3. Perhaps the Persian lions' den resembled some found in Morocco, which "consist of a large square cavern under the earth. . . . The cavern is open above, its mouth being surrounded by a wall of a yard and a half high, over which one can look down into the den." C. F. Keil, *Biblical Commentary on the Book of Daniel*, in *Commentary on the Old Testament*, by C. F. Keil and F. Delitzsch (1959; reprint, Grand Rapids, Mich.: William B. Eerdmans Publishing Co., 1978), vol. 9, p. 216.

4. "The Aramaic together with other early languages has a singularly strong idiom for 'slander,' namely, 'eat the pieces of a man.'" H. C. Leupold, *Exposition of Daniel* (1949; reprint, Grand Rapids, Mich.: Baker Book House, 1969), p. 272.

eaten up themselves. So they, their wives, and their children are tossed into the lions' den (v. 24a). However, the lions do not ignore them like they did Daniel.

They had not reached the bottom of the den before the lions overpowered them and crushed all their bones. (v. 24b)

Finally, Darius reacts *to Daniel's God.* Possibly, through this experience, he became a believer, for he issues a decree to the empire that reflects an unreserved faith in God.

"I make a decree that in all the dominion of my kingdom men are to fear and tremble before the God of Daniel;
  For He is the living God and enduring forever,
  And His kingdom is one which will not be destroyed,
  And His dominion will be forever.
  He delivers and rescues and performs signs and wonders
  In heaven and on earth,
  Who has also delivered Daniel from the power of the lions." (vv. 26–27)

Reminiscent of the God-honoring decree of King Nebuchadnezzar (4:34–35), Darius' edict is a tribute to Daniel's influential, godly character. Through this man of faith (see Heb. 11:32–34), God's name is proclaimed all over the world. And it all began with Daniel's quiet prayers in his bedroom Holy of Holies.

Lasting Lessons That Make the Story Stick

Through Daniel's consistent walk with God and faithful endurance of injustice, he impressed not only the king but the entire kingdom. If we are to have that kind of influence, we need to remember two principles from Daniel's story.

First: *When God proves our faith, He often puts us in difficult places from which we cannot escape.* Like Moses facing the Red Sea with Pharaoh at his back, Daniel faced some deadly lions with no defense and no escape. It's in those types of situations that we must trust God with total abandon. And it's in those situations that God works most spectacularly.

Second: *When God touches those without faith, He often uses our faithful reaction which others cannot ignore.* Were it not for Daniel's faithful trust in God during his predicament, Darius would never have believed. Likewise, our faith while we suffer unjustly often makes an indelible mark on unbelievers who want to know if our God is real.

These two lessons can be summed up in one statement: *The inescapable platform of pain provides the undeniable proof of faith.*

Being unjustly accused and unfairly punished is a painful experience. But when you confront those hungry lions and hear the back door shut behind you, remember that you are not alone. For two faces are watching in the shadows. One is the face of God, who has the power to close the lions' mouths; and the other is the face of a Darius, who desperately wants to know if your beliefs are true. Together, they make two good reasons to endure your suffering with courageous faith.

 Living Insights STUDY ONE

Somewhere in the miles of narrow streets that snake through the Chinese city of Guangzhou (formerly Canton), sixty-year-old Pastor Lam tends his ministry. Twice he has been imprisoned for his faith, the second time for twenty-five years, doing hard labor in the mines. With amazing joy, he recalls those years:

> "It was wonderful! . . . I could have been killed many times, but God preserved my life. And I wasn't injured in the mine, even though men around me were maimed and killed. I even preached there!"[5]

Having faced the lions for more than twenty-five years and survived, Pastor Lam is still stalked by the police. At the thought of a third imprisonment, he laughs out loud and says,

> "I will preach! . . . They can only take me if the Lord lets them. And I will go on preaching about Jesus wherever I am!"[6]

---

5. John White, *Magnificent Obsession*, rev. ed. (Downers Grove, Ill.: InterVarsity Press, 1990), p. 21.

6. White, *Magnificent Obsession*, p. 21.

Pastor Lam is one of many modern Daniels all over the world who practice their faith under fire. Are you in a situation in which others make it difficult for you to express your faith? Describe the circumstances and what it feels like to be put down for your beliefs.

_____

_____

_____

_____

Your suffering for Christ may seem light compared to Pastor Lam's, but regardless of the situation, the joy he experienced can be yours. The key is found in two passages highlighting the apostle Peter. First, read Acts 5:40–42. How did Peter and the other apostles respond after their suffering? Why?

_____

_____

_____

Having himself been tested by adversity, Peter advises others on how to find joy in suffering for Christ. Read 1 Peter 4:12–16. What are the reasons Peter gives for rejoicing during persecution?

_____

_____

_____

Persecution _can_ be a blessing. Daniel found that to be true, as did the apostle Peter and Pastor Lam. You may feel frightened, though, at the thought of suffering for doing right. But God says that enduring hardship for His sake sparks joy. Write a prayer to the Lord, committing yourself to serving Him no matter what; and, like Daniel, don't be afraid to pray with your windows open!

_____

_____

_____

_____

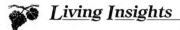 *Living Insights*

Daniel and Darius. One was Hebrew, the other Medean. One worshiped the Lord; the other, pagan gods. Daniel and King Darius would seem to be unlikely candidates for friendship; but in our story, their devotion to one another is inspiring.

From these verses in Daniel 6, what characteristics made their friendship strong?

Verse 3 _____

Verse 14 _____

Verse 16 _____

Verse 18 _____

Verses 20–22 _____

Verses 26–27 _____

Because Daniel refused to isolate himself from unbelieving Darius, the two became friends. And in the end, Darius acknowledged Daniel's God. As Christians, we are wise when we follow Daniel's example, for we need to associate with non-Christians. Jim Petersen has noted:

> It has been observed that the average Christian has no nonChristian friends after he's been a believer for two years. Our contact with the world is then limited to casual acquaintances. We need to relearn how to build relationships with people outside our normal circle of Christian involvement.[7]

If you have felt distant from the non-Christians you know, you can begin developing those acquaintances by incorporating some of the principles from Daniel's friendship with Darius. From the verses you have just examined, select one principle and write down how you can put it into action today.

_____

_____

_____

7. Jim Petersen, *Living Proof* (Colorado Springs, Colo.: NavPress, 1989), p. 54.

Chapter 10

THE CUPBEARER
WHO BUILT A WALL

Selected Passages from Nehemiah

After the crushing Babylonian invasion, the spirit of the Jews lay in ruins like the walls of the city. They had their memories of the grandeur and power of Jerusalem, but that was all. Without walls, the city was defenseless, naked. Without walls the city was not *Jerusalem.*

The task to rebuild was so monumental that even the optimists shook their heads. They needed a leader who could give them a plan and spark a flame of hope that had long been extinguished. That leader had to be just the right person, someone who had connections, someone who had vision, someone who had faith. That someone was Nehemiah.

Living in Persia,[1] far away from Jerusalem, Nehemiah probably never imagined he would be a national hero for his people. However, the Lord had plans for him, not only to rebuild the crumbled walls but also to revive the peoples' spirits. His plan included giving Nehemiah three hats to wear—the subservient hat of cupbearer to the king of Persia, the hard hat of foreman at the construction site, and the dignified hat of a politician, for he became governor of Jerusalem after the wall was complete. Let's take a closer look at each of these three roles.

Cupbearer to the King

As cupbearer for King Artaxerxes (Neh. 1:11b), Nehemiah takes the first sip of the king's wine to protect him against poisoning. But his role goes beyond tasting and serving wine, for he is also a trusted confidant and a respected official who can greatly influence his ruler.

In this position, Nehemiah has reached the pinnacle of success as a foreigner in the Persian court. Yet in his heart, he is unhappy, because he has received disturbing news from his homeland.

---

1. Nehemiah was probably a descendant of the Jews who were exiled after Babylonia destroyed Jerusalem in 586 B.C. He served the Persians because, in 539 B.C., they had conquered the Babylonians.

Now it happened . . . that Hanani, one of my
brothers, and some men from Judah came; and I
asked them concerning the Jews who had escaped
and had survived the captivity, and about Jerusalem.
And they said to me, "The remnant there in the
province who survived the captivity are in great distress and reproach, and the wall of Jerusalem is broken
down and its gates are burned with fire." (Neh. 1:1–3)

Like a brand from that fire, the message burns Nehemiah deep
within his soul. And the only way he knows to quench that smolder-
ing ache is through tears and seeking God on his knees in prayer.

Now it came about when I heard these words, I
sat down and wept and mourned for days; and I was
fasting and praying before the God of heaven. (v. 4)

In his prayer, Nehemiah labors on behalf of the Israelites, plead-
ing for forgiveness of past sins and asking God to bring his people
back together as a nation. He also prays for God's powerful hand
to influence the Persian king to be compassionate toward Israel
(vv. 5–11), knowing that a "king's heart is like channels of water in
the hand of the Lord; / He turns it wherever He wishes" (Prov. 21:1).
After four months[2] of praying and waiting, Nehemiah is serving
wine one day when the king remarks, "Why is your face sad though
you are not sick? This is nothing but sadness of heart" (Neh. 2:2).
Nehemiah feels his heart pound. Never before has he been
downcast in the king's presence. Will Artaxerxes be angry with
him? Will his desire to help God's people be jeopardized?
Mustering his courage, Nehemiah says to the king,

"Let the king live forever. Why should my face not
be sad when the city, the place of my fathers' tombs,
lies desolate and its gates have been consumed by
fire?" (v. 3)

Surprisingly, the king is interested rather than angry. "What
would you request?" he asks (v. 4a).
Whew! Nehemiah breathes easier, but he does not rush his
petition. Instead, he silently "pray[s] to the God of heaven" (v. 4b).
Then he presents his plan to rebuild Jerusalem, including the timing

---

2. *The Living Bible* says in 2:1, "One day in April four months later."

of the project and his need for building supplies and letters of approval (vv. 6–8). Nehemiah has had four long months to think through each detail.

As a result, just as Nehemiah prayed, the king feels compassion for him and his people. As Nehemiah writes in his journal, "And the king granted [my requests] to me because the good hand of my God was on me" (v. 8b).

All is well as he gathers the supplies and is escorted to Judah by a troop of army officers and horsemen (v. 9). But unknown to him, two grumbling officials—Sanballat and Tobiah—have heard about his plan. And "it was very displeasing to them that someone had come to seek the welfare of the sons of Israel" (v. 10b).

Nehemiah's plan has barely started to germinate when the seeds of opposition sprout in the hearts of his enemies. But there is no turning back now. He has put down his cupbearer's hat and reached for his hard hat. Opposition or not, the walls must be built!

Builder of the Wall

When Nehemiah arrives at Jerusalem, he waits three days; then he secretly and systematically examines the ruined walls, evaluating the task ahead (vv. 11–16). Only after he is sure of his strategy does he speak to the people. His journal records the conversation.

> "You see the bad situation we are in, that Jerusalem is desolate and its gates burned by fire. Come, let us rebuild the wall of Jerusalem that we may no longer be a reproach." And I told them how the hand of my God had been favorable to me, and also about the king's words which he had spoken to me. Then they said, "Let us arise and build." So they put their hands to the good work. (vv. 17–18)

Rather than forcing them into action, Nehemiah masterfully motivates the people from within. As he waves the flag of Israel that has been at half-mast for decades, the people rally around it. And their hearts catch fire for Nehemiah's vision as he tells them how the Lord has answered his prayers and moved the heart of King Artaxerxes to send him to them. If God could move a pagan king, He can help them move these stones! So the work begins.

And so does the opposition.

> But when Sanballat the Horonite, and Tobiah the Ammonite official, and Geshem the Arab heard it,

they mocked us and despised us and said, "What is this thing you are doing? Are you rebelling against the king?" (v. 19)

But Nehemiah deflects this criticism.

"The God of heaven will give us success; therefore we His servants will arise and build, but you have no portion, right, or memorial in Jerusalem." (v. 20)

The opposition, however, does not lessen. In fact, it increases when word passes through the region that the walls of Jerusalem are slowly rising out of the rubble, stone by stone (4:1–3). But again, the praying Nehemiah stands firm in the Lord and even encourages the people to defend themselves and fight, if necessary, for their city (vv. 4–14).

Nehemiah's remarkable ability to square off against criticism teaches us three lessons to remember when opposition comes our way.

(1) *It is impossible to lead anyone to do anything without facing opposition.* Criticism is an occupational hazard of leadership.

(2) *It is essential to face opposition first with prayer.* Plugging into God's power bank of wisdom is the most important line of defense, so it's best to do it immediately, before we do anything else.

(3) *It is doubtful that prayer is all that is necessary if the opposition intensifies.* Enemies who relentlessly pelt us are chronic critics; like predictable geysers, they erupt with regular showers of pessimism. In dealing with such critics, God may wish us to defend ourselves by praying *and* taking action.

Most leaders can see overt opposition coming and will raise their shields in defense. Hidden, subverted opposition, however, is more difficult to detect and counter. So when Nehemiah's enemies discover that their frontal assaults are being successfully countered, they decide on a covert plan to destroy Nehemiah and the Jews. And it is cunning.

First, they throw Nehemiah a curveball in the form of a polite letter inviting him to a meeting. But Nehemiah, sensing their treacherous intentions, refuses to come. Not giving up so easily, his enemies throw that same pitch three more times (6:1–4).

Then, frustrated Sanballat sends out a libelous "open letter" for all to see—a beanball pitch, aimed right at Nehemiah's integrity.

In it was written, "It is reported among the nations, and Gashmu says, that you and the Jews are planning to rebel; therefore you are rebuilding the wall. And you are to be their king, according to these reports. And you have also appointed prophets to proclaim in Jerusalem concerning you, 'A king is in Judah!' And now it will be reported to the king according to these reports. So come now, let us take counsel together." (vv. 6–7)

Now trying to frighten him into a meeting, Sanballat accuses Nehemiah of deceitful and selfish intentions. But notice that this crafty enemy quotes no reliable sources and states no solid facts. His purpose is to intimidate, but resting on his blameless record, Nehemiah is not dissuaded from his task.

Then I sent a message to him saying, "Such things as you are saying have not been done, but you are inventing them in your own mind." For all of them were trying to frighten us, thinking, "They will become discouraged with the work and it will not be done." But now, O God, strengthen my hands. (vv. 8–9)

Rather than writing a caustic letter in return, Nehemiah drops to his knees, praying for God's strength. God had overcome tremendous obstacles in bringing him this far, so He can overcome this obstacle as well.

Finally, his enemies resort to their trickiest pitch yet. Nehemiah goes to a friend's house, and this "friend" frantically tells him to run and hide in the temple, for his enemies are coming at night to kill him (v. 10). Shemaiah is a fellow Jew; would he lie? Discerning the truth, Nehemiah answers,

"Should a man like me flee? And could one such as I go into the temple to save his life? I will not go in." Then I perceived that surely God had not sent him, but he uttered his prophecy against me because Tobiah and Sanballat had hired him. (vv. 11–12)

Nehemiah's enemies knew that if they could frighten him into sinning by entering the temple,[3] they would have reason to accuse

---

3. According to Numbers 18:7, priests were allowed near the altar, "but the outsider who comes near shall be put to death."

him (v. 13). But Nehemiah exercises his God-given intuition,[4] perceives their evil plan, and refuses to enter the temple.

Amid the fierce opposition, Nehemiah relies on God's power, and the walls are completed in only fifty-two days (v. 15). That achievement is a tribute to God's strength and impresses even Israel's enemies. But they continue to needle Nehemiah, never giving up their attempts to frighten him (vv. 14–19). Nehemiah's role as builder, however, is finished. He removes his hard hat, but continues to lead the nation in his other role, that of governor.

Governor of the People

Governor Nehemiah is selfless and generous in his position of power (5:14–19), and he builds Israel into a godly nation—a people who treasure the Scriptures (chap. 8), who humble themselves in repentance (chap. 9), and who dedicate the walls and themselves to God (chaps. 10, 12).

The walls and the people become two fitting tributes to Nehemiah's God-honoring leadership. He is a man who, even in the final chapter of his life, is seen building values into the people and seeking God's strength through prayer (chap. 13). In the end, we leave Nehemiah right where we first met him—on his knees, praying (v. 31).

A Few Lessons to Be Learned

Surveying the many events of Nehemiah's life, we come upon three lasting lessons that stand like giant walls of truth.

First: *Dealing with problems begins with careful observation.* Nehemiah had to solve a complex problem—organizing volunteer workers to perform a backbreaking job that had been left undone for decades. It is an example for confronting difficult situations; it begins with careful observation and wise planning.

Second: *Correcting what is carefully observed demands fearless conviction.* The Lord was in Nehemiah's plan; that was why he exhibited such unshakable conviction. Likewise, when we've sought wise counsel and formulated a God-honoring plan, we can and should feel as confident and fearless as Nehemiah, even in the face of opposition.

Third: *Observation and conviction must be tempered with authentic devotion.* We need to devote ourselves to pleasing the Lord through

---

4. *Intuition* is defined as "immediate apprehension . . . quick and ready insight." *Webster's Ninth New Collegiate Dictionary*, see "intuition."

our task. Otherwise, it can become consuming, and we can become cranky and hard-nosed bosses. But by relying on God through prayer, as Nehemiah did, we can maintain our perspective and our love for people.

A Final Thought

Nehemiah was a leader who fought and won his best battles on his knees, in prayer. Critics assailed him relentlessly, but because of his devotion to God, he defeated them on every front.

If you face an enormous task but feel pinned down by chronic critics, remember Nehemiah, whose attitude is best summarized by the inspiring words of Teddy Roosevelt:

> It is not the critic who counts; not the man who points out how the strong man stumbles, or where the doer of deeds could have done them better. The credit belongs to the man who is actually in the arena, whose face is marred by dust and sweat and blood; who strives valiantly; who errs, and comes short again and again, because there is no effort without error and shortcoming; but who does actually strive to do the deeds; who knows the great enthusiasms, the great devotions; who spends himself in a worthy cause; who at the best knows in the end the triumph of high achievement, and who at the worst, if he fails, at least fails while daring greatly, so that his place shall never be with those cold and timid souls who know neither victory nor defeat.[5]

 Living Insights STUDY ONE

Nehemiah endured much enemy fire when he fought to accomplish a great task for the Lord. He dodged bullets on all sides, including mockery, criticism, mudslinging, and physical threats.

---

5. Theodore Roosevelt, from the speech "Citizen in a Republic," given at the Sorbonne in Paris, France, April 23, 1910. As quoted in *The Man In The Arena: Speeches and Essays by Theodore Roosevelt*, ed. John Allen Gable (Oyster Bay, N.Y.: Theodore Roosevelt Association, 1987), p. 54.

Maybe you have been enduring opposition lately. If so, what are the circumstances? Who is against you? How have they been trying to discourage you?

_____

_____

_____

How can you handle that opposition? Nehemiah's example gives three principles for coping with it. The first is: *It's impossible to lead anyone to do anything without facing opposition.* How does it make you feel to know that, if you are a leader, someone *will* oppose you?

_____

_____

Knowing that opposition will come gives you an advantage emotionally. How can accepting the inevitability of criticism give you emotional stability when it comes?

_____

_____

The second principle we studied is: *It's essential to face opposition with prayer.* Turn to three of Nehemiah's short prayers when he was under fire in 4:4–5; 6:9; and 6:14. What did he ask God to do?

_____

_____

Through his prayers, Nehemiah freed himself to concentrate on the task by entrusting his enemies to the Lord. Formulate your own prayer to the Lord, incorporating some ideas from Nehemiah's example.

_____

_____

_____

_____

The third principle on handling opposition is: *It's doubtful that prayer is all that is necessary when opposition intensifies.* Read a good example of this principle in 4:9–14. Nehemiah prayed *and* wisely defended himself and the people. Concerning your situation, what wise actions can you take if the opposition intensifies?

_____

_____

If opposition has you discouraged and retreating, keep in mind the significance of your God-ordained task and remember Nehemiah's words: "The God of heaven will give us success; therefore we His servants will arise and build" (2:20).

 Living Insights

Through the ten stories we have studied in this guide, we've seen victories and we've seen tragedies. But if we just retire these stories to the pages of the Old Testament, they will be nothing more than historical accounts to be dusted off only by scholars and trivia buffs. Instead, we must treasure these stories like a family photo album, reviewing them often and recalling their priceless lessons.

To help you own each story, write down something you gained from it in the space provided. In that way, you will remember the stories, and better yet, you'll be able to pass on what you've learned.

The story of the Israelites and Moses: "The Grumblers Who Died of Snakebite"

_____

_____

The story of Joshua and Jericho: "The City Whose Walls Collapsed"

_____

_____

The story of Achan: "The Man Whose Sin Brought Calamity"

_____

_____

The story of Saul: "The King Who Refused to Bow"

_____

_____

The story of Elijah: "The Prophet Who Prayed to Die"

_____

_____

The story of Naaman: "The Officer Whose Leprosy Was Cleansed"

_____

_____

The story of Gehazi: "The Helper Who Got Greedy"

_____

_____

The story of Elisha and his servant: "The Servant Who Saw the Invisible"

_____

_____

The story of Daniel: "The Commissioner Who Slept with Lions"

_____

_____

The story of Nehemiah: "The Cupbearer Who Built a Wall"

_____

_____

BOOKS FOR
PROBING FURTHER

Roll credits.
Joshua played by Mel Gibson. Gehazi played by Danny DeVito. Jezebel played by Joan Collins. Ahab played by . . . Wait! These stories from the Old Testament aren't movies. They're real life. And the people in the stories are real men and women who walked on our earth and sweltered under our sun. They loved and hurt and laughed and, like us, they encountered God. Some turned away; some knelt in faith. But all were authentic, not caricatures. And we can learn from them.

David C. McCullough has said, "History is a guide to navigation in perilous times."[1] And today, more than ever, we need the guidance biblical history offers. The people we studied in these chapters learned valuable lessons for life, and many of them learned those lessons the hard way. So if we are wise, we will profit from their mistakes and prosper from their discoveries.

The following resources expand on the major themes addressed in the stories we studied. As you peruse the list, don't be overwhelmed by the number of titles—just choose the one or two that most apply to your present situation. With that book and your Bible open to the applicable story, let history and God's Spirit be your guides to navigating the days ahead.

Facing Obstacles

Spangler, Ann and Charles Turner, eds. *Heroes.* Ann Arbor, Mich.: Servant Publications, Vine Books, 1983, 1985. "Who is your hero?" That was the question posed to twenty respected Christian leaders, and their compiled answers make up this book. The heroes they selected range from Mother Teresa to Blaise Pascal, and they all tell inspiring stories of how courageous people through history have remained faithful to the Lord, against all odds.

---

1. David C. McCullough, in *Simpson's Contemporary Quotations,* comp. James B. Simpson (Boston, Mass.: Houghton Mifflin Co., 1988), p. 234.

Swindoll, Charles R. *Hand Me Another Brick.* Nashville, Tenn.: Thomas Nelson Publishers, 1978. This book about the "cup-bearer who built a wall" goes into much more detail about the life and lessons of Nehemiah. Here you'll find brick after brick for building solid, biblical leadership qualities in your life, and you'll learn how to keep the construction going in the face of inevitable opposition and obstacles.

Dealing with Sin

Miller, J. Keith. *Sin: Overcoming the Ultimate Deadly Addiction.* San Francisco, Calif.: Harper and Row, Publishers, 1987. Achan, Saul, and Gehazi suffered because of the effects of sin in their lives. In this book, Miller explains how sinful behavior can become an addiction, how to confront it head-on, and how to manage it through God's strength. The tragic lives of sin-diseased characters in the Bible warn us of sin's effects. Don't let sin run out of control in your life too.

Mosley, Steven. *There I Go Again.* Dallas, Tex.: Word Publishing, 1991. Subtitled *How to Keep from Falling for the Same Old Sin,* this book hits home with practical advice for all Christians. Mosley is personal and honest, giving biblical truths for fighting sin instead of always giving in.

Change

White, John. *Changing on the Inside.* Ann Arbor, Mich.: Servant Publications, Vine Books, 1991. God cleansed Naaman's leprosy as well as his sinful heart. But it took humble obedience and repentance on Naaman's part to experience that change. The same is true for us. And once we believe, God continues the process of change—from the inside.

Stress and Depression

Cloud, Henry. *When Your World Makes No Sense.* Nashville, Tenn.: Thomas Nelson Publishers, Oliver Nelson, 1990. The author writes about four aspects of our personality that influence our well-being: the needs to bond, to have boundaries, to resolve problems, and to establish authority over our lives as adults. As we fulfill these needs through our relationship with God, we are on our way to stability and wholeness.

Hart, Archibald D. *Adrenalin and Stress*. Waco, Tex.: Word Books, 1988. Elijah's depression developed out of a high-stress situation. If we are to guard ourselves against an Elijah-like depression, then we need to learn to handle stress. Thoroughly exploring that subject, Hart helps you understand the effects of stress and suggests ways to manage them.

White, John. *The Masks of Melancholy*. Downers Grove, Ill.: Inter-Varsity Press, 1982. As a physician, White looks you in the eye and gives you the straight facts about depression and suicide. His book is a valuable tool for anyone who is longing to understand and encourage a depressed friend or relative.

Devotion to Christ

Stedman, Ray. *Authentic Christianity*. Portland, Oreg.: Multnomah Press, 1975. A man of steadfast, authentic faith, Daniel stood for God against his times—a stand that resulted in a worldly king decreeing, "in all the dominion of my kingdom men are to fear and tremble before the God of Daniel" (Dan. 6:26a). In this book by Ray Stedman, you will learn through the wisdom of 2 Corinthians how you can model Daniel's same faith and draw lost souls to the saving glory of Christ who shines through you.

White, John. *Magnificent Obsession*. Revised edition. Downers Grove, Ill.: InterVarsity Press, 1990. A revised edition of White's earlier work *The Cost of Commitment* (InterVarsity, 1976), this book reflects the author's growth, maturity, and increased passion for Christ. In his preface he writes: "Commitment to Christ is commitment to the pursuit of the ultimate treasure." White invites you to pursue this ultimate treasure with him, a treasure which Daniel found worth facing a den of lions for . . . a treasure which will never lose its worth.

ORDERING INFORMATION

Cassette Tapes and Study Guide

This Bible study guide was designed to be used independently or in conjunction with the broadcast of Chuck Swindoll's taped messages on the topic listed below. If you would like to order cassette tapes or further copies of this study guide, please see the information given below and the Order Form provided on the last page of this guide.

GREAT STORIES
FROM OLD TESTAMENT LIVES

We live in a world of facts and faxes, spread sheets and the bottom line. When do we have time to read a good story?

We used to have time. As children, we would step into a land of heroes and giants, evil kings and conniving queens. Wouldn't it be wonderful to rediscover the excitement of those stories?

You can if you open up the greatest storybook ever written—the Bible. For here you'll find heroes like David, giants like Goliath, evil kings like Ahab, and conniving queens like Jezebel. And best of all, you'll find truths to help you cope in this world—your world, which can be made richer by a few great stories from the Old Testament.

			Calif.*	U.S.	B.C.*	Canada*
GSL	SG	Study Guide	$ 4.24	$ 3.95	$ 5.08	$ 5.08
GSL	CS	Cassette series, includes album cover	31.64	29.50	45.01	42.76
GSL	1–5	Individual cassettes, include messages A and B	5.36	5.00	7.61	7.23

*These prices already include the following charges: for delivery in **California,** applicable sales tax; **Canada,** 7% GST and 7% postage and handling (on tapes only); **British Columbia,** 7% GST, 6% British Columbia sales tax (on tapes only), and 7% postage and handling (on tapes only). **The prices are subject to change without notice.**

GSL 1-A: *The Grumblers Who Died of Snakebite*—Numbers 21:4–9
       B: *The City Whose Walls Collapsed*—Joshua 5:13–6:21

GSL 2-A: *The Man Whose Sin Brought Calamity*—Joshua 7
       B: *The King Who Refused to Bow*—1 Samuel 13–15

GSL 3-A: *The Prophet Who Prayed to Die*—1 Kings 19:1–14, 18–21
B: *The Officer Whose Leprosy Was Cleansed*—2 Kings 5:1–14
GSL 4-A: *The Helper Who Got Greedy*—2 Kings 5:15–16, 19–27
B: *The Servant Who Saw the Invisible*—2 Kings 6:8–20
GSL 5-A: *The Commissioner Who Slept with Lions*—Daniel 6
B: *The Cupbearer Who Built a Wall*—Selected Passages from Nehemiah

How to Order by Mail

Simply mark on the order form whether you want the series or individual tapes. Mail the form with your payment to the appropriate address listed below. We will process your order as promptly as we can.

United States: Mail your order to the Sales Department at Insight for Living, Post Office Box 69000, Anaheim, California 92817-0900. If you wish your order to be shipped first-class for faster delivery, add 10 percent of the total order amount. Otherwise, please allow four to six weeks for delivery by fourth-class mail. We accept personal checks, money orders, Visa, or MasterCard in payment for materials. Unfortunately, we are unable to offer invoicing or COD orders.

Canada: Mail your order to Insight for Living Ministries, Post Office Box 2510, Vancouver, British Columbia V6B 3W7. Allow approximately four weeks for delivery. We accept personal checks, money orders, Visa, or MasterCard in payment for materials. Unfortunately, we are unable to offer invoicing or COD orders.

Australia, New Zealand, or Papua New Guinea: Mail your order to Insight for Living, Inc., GPO Box 2823 EE, Melbourne, Victoria 3001, Australia. Please allow six to ten weeks for delivery by surface mail. If you would like your order sent airmail, the delivery time may be reduced. Using the United States price as a base, add postage costs—surface or airmail—to the amount of your order. Please use the chart that follows to determine correct postage. Due to fluctuating currency rates, we can accept only personal checks made payable in U.S. funds, international money orders, Visa, or MasterCard in payment for materials.

Overseas: Other overseas residents should mail their orders to our United States office. Please allow six to ten weeks for delivery by surface mail. If you would like your order sent airmail, the delivery time may be reduced. Using the United States price as a base, add postage costs—surface or airmail—to the amount of your order. Please use the chart that follows to determine correct postage. Due to fluctuating currency rates, we can accept only personal checks made payable in U.S. funds, international money orders, Visa, or MasterCard in payment for materials.

Type of Postage	Postage Cost
Surface	10% of total order
Airmail	25% of total order

For Faster Service, Order by Telephone or FAX

For Visa or MasterCard orders, you are welcome to use one of our toll-free numbers between the hours of 7:00 A.M. and 4:30 P.M., Pacific time, Monday through Friday, or our FAX numbers. The numbers to use from anywhere in the United States are **1-800-772-8888** or FAX (714) 575-5049. To order from Canada, call our Vancouver office using **1-800-663-7639** or FAX (604) 596-2975. Vancouver residents, call (604) 596-2910. Australian residents should phone (03) 872-4606. From other international locations, call our Sales Department at (714) 575-5000 in the United States.

Our Guarantee

Our cassettes are guaranteed for ninety days against faulty performance or breakage due to a defect in the tape. For best results, please be sure your tape recorder is in good operating condition and is cleaned regularly.

Note: To cover processing and handling, there is a $10 fee for *any* returned check.

Insight for Living Catalog

Request a free copy of the Insight for Living catalog of books, tapes, and study guides by calling **1-800-772-8888** in the United States or **1-800-663-7639** in Canada.

Order Form

GSL CS represents the entire *Great Stories from Old Testament Lives* series in a special album cover, while GSL 1–5 are the individual tapes included in the series. GSL SG represents this study guide, should you desire to order additional copies.

Item	Calif.*	Unit Price U.S.	B.C.*	Canada*	Quantity	Amount
GSL CS	$31.64	$29.50	$45.01	$42.76		$
GSL 1	5.36	5.00	7.61	7.23		
GSL 2	5.36	5.00	7.61	7.23		
GSL 3	5.36	5.00	7.61	7.23		
GSL 4	5.36	5.00	7.61	7.23		
GSL 5	5.36	5.00	7.61	7.23		
GSL SG	4.24	3.95	5.08	5.08		
					Subtotal	
					Overseas Residents *Pay U.S. price plus 10% surface postage or 25% airmail. Also, see "How to Order by Mail."*	
					U.S. First-Class Shipping *For faster delivery, add 10% for postage and handling.*	
					Gift to Insight for Living *Tax-deductible in the United States and Canada.*	
					Total Amount Due *Please do not send cash.*	$

If there is a balance: ☐ apply it as a donation ☐ please refund
*These prices already include applicable taxes and shipping costs.

Payment by: ☐ Check or money order made payable to Insight for Living or

☐ Credit card (circle one): Visa MasterCard   Number _____

   Expiration Date _____ Signature _____
                                             We cannot process your credit card purchase without your signature.

Name _____

Address _____

City _____ State/Province _____

Zip/Postal Code _____ Country _____

Telephone (____)_____ Radio Station ___ ___ ___ ___
         If questions arise concerning your order, we may need to contact you.

Mail this order form to the Sales Department at one of these addresses:

Insight for Living, Post Office Box 69000, Anaheim, CA 92817-0900
Insight for Living Ministries, Post Office Box 2510, Vancouver, BC, Canada V6B 3W7
Insight for Living, Inc., GPO Box 2823 EE, Melbourne, VIC 3001, Australia